"They reach out to us across the centuries. T[...] our weary souls. Just as a sovereign God transformed their lives, their stories ignite transformation in ours. These women of the Bible—our sisters—still 'walk beside us.'

"Join Lisa and Dawn as they invite us into a dialogue, a relationship, a life-changing odyssey with these special women. Leaders, in a time when women were not, we can learn valuable lessons from their lives.

"A must-read for every woman trying to balance and juggle the demands of a hectic life, trying to seek the heart of God, and trying to become the woman, the leader, He created her to be."

—Dr. Cynthia Fantasia, Grace Chapel; Lexington, MA

"Have you ever felt intimidated or irritated with the Proverbs 31 woman? In *Real Women Leading: With Proverbs 31 Values*, authors Lisa Troyer and Dawn Yoder reveal the powerful principles that dispel myths and reveal truth. This book is for every woman who longs to live out her values and faith in the middle of an intensely busy life. Each chapter weaves essential truth with poignant examples from biblical women and contemporary stories. The value-added "IT Factor" section will propel you in the direction of transformational living as you become intentional about your choices. This is a powerful read!"

—Carol Kent, speaker and best-selling author of *Becoming a Woman of Influence* and *Unquenchable: Grow a Wildfire Faith that Will Endure Anything*

"Solomon's 700 wives couldn't live up to the elusive Proverbs 31 woman . . . and I feared I never would either. Lisa and Dawn interpret this passage for *Real Women Leading: With Proverbs 31 Values*, vividly illustrating how these timeless principles play out in modern families, on the job, and in our communities. Their practical 'Steps to Follow' in each chapter guide women into rich relationships and positions of influence that value their God-given strengths and further God's kingdom. This book offers a fresh translation on merchant ships and maids, distaffs and spindles that today's real woman can truly understand and actually apply."

—AMY LIVELY, creator of the Neighborhood Cafe

"They get it! Lisa and Dawn show believing women how to integrate their faith and influence into their real lives."

—LINDA EVANS SHEPHERD, author of *Experiencing God's Presence: Learning to Listen While You Pray*

"Lisa and Dawn have offered a fresh tool to the entire kingdom of God. The word pictures (i.e., damp matches) and suggestions for leadership are extremely valuable, regardless of gender, and the insights from the Word with practical applications cross over into a variety of leadership arenas. I am grateful for how this resource will impact the effectiveness of our leaders."

—BRENDA MASON YOUNG, Cornerstone Church; director, Clear Blue Global Water Project

REAL WOMEN LEADING

WITH PROVERBS

31

VALUES

LISA TROYER AND
DAWN YODER

NEW HOPE
PUBLISHERS
Gospel-Centered. Missions-Driven.

BIRMINGHAM, ALABAMA

New Hope® Publishers
PO Box 12065
Birmingham, AL 35202-2065
NewHopeDigital.com
New Hope Publishers is a division of WMU®.

Library of Congress Control Number: 2013952369

All Scripture quotations, unless otherwise indicated, are taken from the HOLY BIBLE, NEW INTERNATIONAL VERSION®. NIV®. Copyright ©1973, 1978, 1984 by International Bible Society. Used by permission of Zondervan. All rights reserved.

Scripture quotations marked *The Message* are taken from *The Message* by Eugene H. Peterson. Copyright © 1993, 1994, 1995, 1996, 2000, 2001, 2002. Used by permission of NavPress Publishing Group."

Scripture quotations marked AMP are taken from the Amplified® Bible, Copyright © 1954, 1958, 1962, 1964, 1965, 1987 by The Lockman Foundation. Used by permission.

Scripture quotations marked NLT are taken from the *Holy Bible,* New Living Translation, copyright © 1996. Used by permission of Tyndale House Publishers, Inc., Wheaton, Illinois. All rights reserved.

Scripture quotations marked ESV are from The Holy Bible, English Standard Version, copyright © 2001 by Crossway Bibles, a division of Good News Publishers. Used by permission. All rights reserved.

Scripture quotations marked NKJV are taken from the New King James Version. Copyright © 1982 by Thomas Nelson, Inc. Used by permission. All rights reserved.

ISBN-10: 1-59669-396-7
ISBN-13: 978-1-59669-396-8
N144105 • 0214 • 3M

Concepts and format for "The IT Factor" portions of this book were inspired by the Global Priority Roundtable Principles©, copyright 2013, and were used by permission. For more information, go to globalpriority.org.

TABLE OF CONTENTS

DEDICATION

To my husband *Bob,* and our children, *Jillian* and *Christian.* I could not ask for a more loving and supportive family. I'm blessed to live my life in your presence. Knowing that Christ is the center of our lives and our home is "heaven on earth."

— *Lisa Troyer*

———

To my husband, *Jeff,* and my children, *Austin, Mason, Jaxon,* and *London,* for your steady support, encouragement, and belief in me. Aside from salvation, you are God's greatest blessings in my life.

— *Dawn Yoder*

Acknowledgments

My appreciation and gratitude goes out to *Carol Kent* and *Andrea Mullins.* Wonderful women of God, and leaders who are examples to all who follow God's call to mentor and minister to the body of Christ.

To *Missy Horsfall* and *Tanya Glanzman,* your assistance and participation in this project have been invaluable.

To my parents, *Peter* and *Nancy Dauwalder,* for the lessons in life and business, that being generous is its own reward, and that God's Word never returns void. He honors those who step out in faith to make their communities a catalyst for creativity and inspiration. Thank you for telling me that a daughter could not only be a blessing to her family, but also to other families around the world.

— Lisa Troyer

My gratitude goes out to my mentors, *Dr. John Maxwell, Mike Poulin,* and *Bernie Torrence,* for teaching me about leadership, values, and connecting with people.

To my parents, *Jerri* and *Jerry Anderson,* thank you, Mom and Dad, for teaching me about faith and values and for showing me how applying God's values makes life work. Thank you for being role models for me by demonstrating how to walk in faith and how to recover when you fail.

A special word of appreciation to the *Global Priority* organization for allowing us to use your values-based material as a springboard for the ideas in this book. Thank you for the privilege of working with you as writers and trainers to affect the world for the kingdom of God.

— Dawn Yoder

FOREWORD

I have gotten to know Dawn Yoder and Lisa Troyer over the past few years as they have been mentored by me as founding members of the John Maxwell Team. The John Maxwell Team is an elite organization of coaches, teachers, and speakers from around the world who are eager to learn and grow in the area of leadership. They came to our team because they have a passion for personal growth and for adding value to others. These two just love people. They love encouraging them, challenging them, and cheering on their development. They want to be people who are making a difference doing something that makes a difference with other people who are making a difference. They are leaders in business and ministry while also making family a priority. Over the years, I've come to appreciate their communication skills as teachers and trainers and their commitment to biblical leadership principles. They have a passion for values because they see what a difference living by values has made in their own businesses, families, and life.

Dawn and Lisa are both involved in my nonprofit organization, EQUIP. EQUIP is committed to training and developing millions of godly leaders throughout the world in support of the Great Commission. Lisa has made several trips to Germany and Switzerland to invest in the people and has joined EQUIP with plans of doing future trips with us there. Dawn worked with EQUIP in June 2013 on a nationwide initiative called Transformation Is in Me, in Guatemala. This initiative was set up to empower the people of Guatemala to bring transformation to their country through the application of values and personal growth. She was one of the primary content developers and trainers for that extremely successful kickoff. She trained 140 of our coaches from the John Maxwell Team who then trained more than 14,000 people in three days to lead their own transformation groups in their sphere of influence. As of November 2013, there were more than 58,000 Guatemalan people involved in transformation groups and the numbers are growing by the week. Dawn continues to function as a trainer of trainers within EQUIP.

You may ask yourself, *John Maxwell is a leadership teacher, what does that have to do with values?* The answer is simple, in order to lead others well, you must first lead yourself well. You cannot lead yourself well without good character. I live by a "Rule of 5" — five things I endeavor to do every day without fail. One of the five things on my daily agenda is adding value to others. Every day, I make a conscious effort to add value to the people around me. I have come to realize that living by values is a key to accomplishing this. I challenge you to find a way to add value to others without first having internalized concepts like understanding people, humility, and generosity. It can't be done. You have to be a person who lives by values if you want to add value to others.

Values affect every area of our life. They affect every decision we make, how we treat other people, and how other people respond to us. No person is an island. Everything we do affects the people around us. That is why it is important to have a strong internal compass to guide us as we are navigating the many decisions we make every day. If we embrace a value and internalize it, it becomes a part of our navigation system guiding us to wise choices. Wise choices lead us to personal success and favor with others.

When you make a conscientious effort to apply anything in your life, you will see that area flourish. It doesn't matter what it is . . . working on communication skills, developing your leadership ability, learning an instrument, training for a race . . . focus, application, and discipline will bring growth. It is no different with our character. Focused time on character will cause our character to grow and become stronger. If you fail to focus on it, it can start to slip.

I often hear people talk about core values. Those are the values that are intrinsic to them, the nonnegotiables of life. When you break the phrase down, the first part of it is core. Core is the central and most essential part of something. Physically, our core, the center part of our body, is what physicians recommend we work on to stay strong and fit. But our core will not stay strong by doing a few sit ups here and there. We have to work it. It takes daily focus and discipline to get a strong core. It is the same with values. If we want the core of our character to remain strong, we need to focus and discipline ourselves to be aware of and working on our character. I have often said that character growth determines the height of our personal growth. Without personal growth, we will never be able to reach our potential or fulfill the destiny God has set before us. People want to follow leaders with good character. No one likes to work with or even be close friends with unreliable people. Good character, with honesty and integrity at its core, is essential to success in any area of life.

Often, people have a tendency to focus too much on competence and too little on character. Being intentional in developing our character is necessary and totally within our control. When it comes to our talents and abilities, we need to focus on working on our strengths knowing that when we work at something we are already good at, we will experience immediate growth and rise quickly in our field. It is just the opposite when it comes to our character. With character, we need to focus on our weakness because our weakness is what has the potential to undo any good we could do and may even end up dismantling our lives if it goes unchecked. It is like constructing a building on an unstable foundation . . . eventually you will have major problems.

As you read through this book, I encourage you to reflect and then quickly apply what you learn because biblically based values have the potential to dramatically transform your life. Use "The IT Factor" at the end of each chapter to evaluate how well you are doing on that character quality and to form a measureable action step that will enable you to immediately apply and grow in that value.

God is *the* greatest visionary leader of all time. Great leaders have a heart for their people and give them everything they need to succeed. They set direction, expose the big picture, provide support, and hold their followers responsible. That is exactly what God has done for us. He gave us the Bible, the best-selling book of all time, to teach us how to live a successful life. This book, *Real Women Leading: With Proverbs 31 Values*, helps you to really dig into the direction that God has already provided and gives practical application for everyday life.

— DR. JOHN C. MAXWELL

johnmaxwell.com

INTRODUCTION

The Proverbs 31 woman. Whether we love her, hate her, fear her, admire or revere her, we view her as the original woman to "bring home the bacon and fry it up in a pan." This lyric from a late 1970s perfume commercial jingle became the anthem of the trending independent, I-can-do-it-all woman. That was quite a departure from the iconic June Cleaver of the previous generation, the stay-at-home mother in the television show *Leave It to Beaver* who, in a dress, high heels, and pearls (even while vacuuming), consistently and graciously met the needs of her husband and sons.

The commercial jingle reflected western society's belief that the women's liberation movement ushered in the possibility of women having it all — a fulfilling family life and a presence in the marketplace, as well as respect from her husband, children, and community. But the Bible had western society beat by thousands of years!

It is ironic that the activities which society at one time perceived as rebellion are actually what God planned all along. God had it figured out — He intended that a woman receive respect and honor for her life choices. Living out our full potential was not something we were intended to have to fight for, defend, apologize for, or hide.

Often thought of as the "most intimidating woman in Christendom," perhaps the Proverbs 31 woman — this skillful, conscientious, generous, creative, entrepreneurial, merciful leader — has been saddled with a false persona of perfectionism and unattainable achievement.

The Proverbs 31 woman was not someone I wanted to read about when I was a girl. The way she was presented just made me mad. All that talk about sewing clothes, cooking breakfast early in the morning, and taking care of fields held no interest for me whatsoever. The focus was on being a homemaker and a good, submissive wife, while my most hated word at that time was *submission*. Rebellion, anyone? As a teenage girl in a fundamental church, I recall reading and hearing about her in a women's meeting and wanting desperately to find a way to exit the building or mentally "check out." I did not want to be someone's pretty, little slave.

Maybe my attitude came from being raised in a family business and having an achiever mentality. I was never interested in or very good at working behind the scenes. The idea of making a house run like clockwork and waiting on everyone hand and foot while my husband went out to change the world could not have been less appealing. I did not see any way that I could possibly be like the woman in Proverbs 31. Since I thought I did not want what God had in mind, I felt destined to be "less than" — less than this virtuous woman, less than what a woman should be, less than what God wanted me to be. I believed in the literal interpretation of the passage and missed its underlying message. Trying to emulate this seemingly unachievable model made me feel defeated, so I lacked the desire to try.

My mom has always said that my only domestic quality is that I live in a house. Before you judge her parenting too harshly, you must know that my mom is amazing, and she was and is 100 percent correct. Mom knows me well. She knows what makes my heart sing. She knows the areas I am gifted in, and her saying that released me from feeling I had to be the "domestic goddess" I am not cut out to be. I hate to cook, I am not a morning person, I know nothing about farming or fields, and the thought of sewing my own clothes is completely foreign (and terrifying) to me.

However, God has given me many gifts and talents. I take care of my family. I am a businesswoman. I love to work with people and help them develop to their fullest potential. I am active in my church and in ministry. Some people have even said they think of me as a Proverbs 31 woman! I used to laugh and think they must not know me very well, but then I decided maybe she deserved a second look. So, as a real, live, grown-up girl, I looked to see if I had more in common with her than I had once thought. What I discovered is that we all have more in common with her than we might think. I simply had never realized what God intended for women.

The picture we see in Proverbs 31 is a woman who is honest, trustworthy, and generous. A good steward, she has fun and makes fun, is a good planner, and maintains a good attitude. She understands people, prepares for the future, shows restraint, and likes to put together a nice outfit. This chick is awesome and leaves the rest of us a lot to live up to. Looking at her this way, she is no longer someone I am afraid I could never be. She is now someone I *want* to be! The Proverbs 31 woman finds success everywhere she turns because she lives by God's principles. Because she does the things that make life work, she finds favor and security in every area of her life.

God's encouragement to us is this: He has given us all we need to be what He has called us to be, if we do it in and through Him.

— *Dawn*

The truth is, we can all be like the Proverbs 31 woman, just not the one who has been the iconic standard — as she's been portrayed. We can emulate the role demonstrated by this heroine of Scripture because the Bible never encourages us to attempt something unattainable. God is not the author of confusion, nor is He intimidated by our shortcomings. Maybe the reason so few women sense they can live (and lead) this way is that interpretations of these verses too often miss the values and principles they set forth.

Has the church at times been slow to deliver the encouragement and fellowship that is so desperately needed by women in the marketplace? Or is it having difficulty meeting them where they are? Many women who are called to a more domestic vocation are available for the Tuesday morning Bible study offered by the local church. But an increasing percentage of the female population in our culture is spending those hours at a workplace. For instance, a 2013 Pew Research poll indicates that 40 percent of the women who work outside the home do it not merely to add income to the family budget but are the main breadwinners for their families (necessitating more hours at work). In 1960 that number was only 11 percent.

Sadly, an air of condescension sometimes seeps into the hearts and minds of women who do not have the same experience in today's challenging and often competitive world. Whether we are homeschooling children — which truly is a full-time vocation — or leading the board of directors meeting at a Fortune 500 corporation, the Proverbs 31 woman has something to teach all of us. Let's consider her attributes.

She is humble. She realizes that preparedness and delegation are two essential ingredients of success. She is not expecting to do it all; she knows how to delegate responsibility while encouraging others to walk in their own gifts. She is extremely industrious. In her wisdom, however, she realizes that the success she desires — as well as the appreciation of her family, friends, and business associates — is best facilitated by drawing people together and connecting them, bringing everyone's talent into the mix.

She finds others who, like her, are responsible, influential, and ambitious. Then she proceeds to use her values-based influence to grow the virtues of honesty, generosity, and restraint. This not only makes life work better for her family but also for those who, by following her example, are developing their own skill sets.

With many women in today's culture as part of the workforce, the potential to change the environments of the households to which they retreat in the evening is incredible. Perhaps, this could be likened to the vision-driven creator of the first spacecraft to venture to the moon. This was a person who saw the potential to go where no man had gone before and also had the hope and belief that the means to get there could be developed.

Although we're certainly not comparing this book to manned spaceflight, we hope that in it you will find the voices of real women, some from Scripture and some contemporary, speaking to us about the real issues we all face. And we hope you'll gain from their insight.

> Growing up in a family business environment, for me it's not an either/or proposition — it's both/and. I am a wife, mom, daughter, executive, marketer, and manager. Sometimes I am delegating, sometimes I am "bringing home the bacon," sometimes I am the hostess to family and friends, sometimes I am the mom nursing the fevered child in the middle of the night, and sometimes I am the woman who is intentionally stealing a few romantic moments with my husband. It's a good life, it's a challenging life, and it's a principled life. It's a life that

God blesses because He knows that I trust Him with the time and the opportunity He's placed in my hands.

— *Lisa*

A LIFE GOD CAN BLESS

Proverbs 31 is really a description of every woman — maybe even all women at the same time. Let's face it, the woman was an incredible multitasker! By listing so many activities in so many areas, the Bible shows us that it isn't so much about *what* we do as *how* we do it. The woman in Proverbs 31 exhibits principle and character. This Scripture shows that she operates with integrity and is a good steward of everything God puts in her hand. Let's look at what the passage is telling us.

> *The heart of her husband trusts in her confidently and relies on and believes in her securely, so that he has no lack of [honest] gain or need of [dishonest] spoil* (v. 11).

Her husband trusts her judgment. He relies on her to sort out the difference between emotion and fact and to use her discernment to help. *The Message* puts it this way: "Her husband trusts her without reserve and never has reason to regret it."

> *She comforts, encourages, and does him only good as long as there is life within her* (v. 12).

Her heart is for him. She wants to help bring out the best in him and help him to reach his God-given potential. The New Living Translation

(NLT) says she brings him "good, not harm" and *The Message* says she "treats him generously all her life long."

> *She seeks out wool and flax and works with willing*
> *hands [to develop it]* (v. 13).

She looks for quality wherever she goes and then sets her mind to add value to it. (Some translations describe this as working with eager hands and with delight.) This woman enjoys finding the best deals and working to accomplish her goal.

> *She is like the merchant ships loaded with foodstuffs; she*
> *brings her household's food from a far [country]* (v. 14).

She looks for the best things to bring into her household to help her family develop into all they can be. She provides her family with healthy food, a safe home, medical attention, good entertainment, and fun. And she also helps family members discover what they are good at, develop spiritually, and complete schoolwork.

> *She rises while it is yet night and gets [spiritual] food for*
> *her household and assigns her maids their tasks* (v. 15).

She makes good use of her time and makes sure things are taken care of through wise planning. She is not a martyr. She does not try to do it all herself but delegates work to get things done efficiently and to help others develop their skills.

> *She considers a [new] field before she buys or accepts*
> *it [expanding prudently and not courting neglect of*

her present duties by assuming other duties]; with her
savings [of time and strength] she plants fruitful vines in
her vineyard (v. 16).

She keeps an open mind to new opportunities but weighs out the pros
and cons before she takes advantage of them. She has the courage
to say yes but is not afraid to say no. She makes sure she takes care
of what is entrusted to her — whether it is her family or corporate
resources — and develops them fully.

She girds herself with strength [spiritual, mental, and
physical fitness for her God-given task] and makes her
arms strong and firm (v. 17).

She takes care of herself physically and spiritually and looks for ways
to learn and grow. Her attention to the physical is not a quest for
perfection or for vanity's sake but so that she can be her best self to
care for those around her. Spiritually, she is rooted in God's Word
and finds her strength, peace, self-worth, and answers in God.

She tastes and *sees that her gain from work [with and*
for God] is good; her lamp goes not out, but it burns on
continually through the night [of trouble, privation, or
sorrow, warning away fear, doubt, and distrust] (v. 18).

She celebrates victories and makes it a point to remember all that God
has done to carry her through trying circumstances.

She lays her hands to the spindle, and her hands hold
the distaff (v. 19).

She is a hard worker. *The Message* describes her as one who "senses the worth of her work."

> *She opens her hand to the poor, yes, she reaches out her filled hands to the needy [whether in body, mind, or spirit] (v. 20).*

She is generous to others and seeks to provide the things they really need and not just what they think they need (acting as an enabler) or what is convenient for her to give. She listens to and understands people well.

> *She fears not the snow for her family, for all her household are doubly clothed in scarlet (v. 21).*

She is a big-picture thinker. She looks ahead to see what is coming next. She makes sure real needs are met and refuses to worry about the rest.

> *She makes for herself coverlets, cushions, and rugs of tapestry. Her clothing is of linen, pure and fine, and of purple [such as that of which the clothing of the priests and the hallowed cloths of the temple were made] (v. 22).*

She makes the most of all she has and is not afraid to wear her best or make herself and her home look as nice as she can. In other words, it is not frivolous or ridiculous to try and make the most of what you've got — actually, it's good stewardship.

> *Her husband is known in the [city's] gates, when he sits among the elders of the land (v. 23).*

She makes her husband look good; she adds value to who he is. She honors him with both her actions and her words. This brings him favor among his peers and co-workers.

> She makes fine linen garments and leads others to buy them; she delivers to the merchant's girdles [or sashes that free one up for service] (v. 24).

She uses all of her God-given talents, wherever that leads her. If you are good at selling, then sell! Do not be afraid to use your talents. It honors the Lord when you use the gifts He has placed within you for good things.

> Strength and dignity are her clothing and her position is strong and secure; she rejoices over the future [the latter day or time to come, knowing that she and her family are in readiness for it]! (v. 25).

She is secure in who she is because she knows whose she is. She operates with godly principles and has a positive attitude because she knows God is in control. She can trust that, as she walks in His ways, He is both trustworthy and never failing.

> She opens her mouth in skillful and godly Wisdom, and on her tongue is the law of kindness [giving counsel and instruction] (v. 26).

She speaks affirming words and gives good advice. She speaks out of what she knows—and she is purposeful to know God's Word and display a heart of love for others.

She looks well to how things go in her household, and the bread of idleness (gossip, discontent, and self-pity) she will not eat (v. 27).

She does not waste time feeling sorry for herself or gossiping about others. When she is tempted to speak negative or hurtful words, she shows restraint. Her thoughts are focused on what she has and what she can do, rather than on what she lacks or the ways others fall short Proverbs 31:11–27 (AMP; with authors' interpretation).

Each of our experiences is unique. Some of us have experiences that come from having little privilege, and some of us have experiences from having much. We are all, however, created with a God-given purpose. Each of us has the ability to be a woman of influence. Being a woman of positive influence, like the Proverbs 31 woman, is based on living a life built on wisdom and principled thinking and application.

God's personality is not one-dimensional and, being made in His image, neither is ours. We are diverse and brimming with incredible potential. Join us on this journey of discovering more about the principles shared by the Proverbs 31 woman. Ask God to speak to you directly and believe that He will. He's willing, ready, and waiting to reveal to you how He has already equipped you for a purposeful and fulfilling life this side of eternity.

In the following chapters we will look at ten of the foundational principles found in Proverbs 31: understanding people, forgiveness, responsibility, attitude, resolving conflict, restraint, honesty, planning, generosity, and influence. Developing these traits in our lives will lead us to become the women God designed us to be.

A heart that utilizes every gift and opportunity the way God intends acts as a conduit for the potential God has placed inside each of us. We could even be vessels created for "such a time as this" (Esther 4:14). As you read, study, discuss, and apply the principles in this book, carefully consider what God has placed in your hand. Every gift, relationship, and opportunity you have is something in your hand to be used to further God's kingdom.

IGNITING TRANSFORMATION — THE IT FACTOR

Each chapter will conclude with a section called "The IT Factor," designed to prompt thought, conversation, and action concerning the value focused on within that chapter.

As we begin to develop our skills to implement biblical values and principles where God gives us opportunity and influence, we need to ask, *Why is this so important?*

We all have a divine purpose for our lives, a reason God has placed us in this time and place we live and work. What is your mission? Do you see yourself as a catalyst to bring lasting change and kingdom activity to the areas that you visit daily? When interacting with your family, co-workers, church family, and greater community, is your goal to further your own agenda or is it to bring transformation? The value of a life well-lived is having an impact on those whom you have the opportunity to interact with regularly.

Often we hear, "There needs to be a change." But that is as far as it goes. We see the need, but we are so encumbered by our own goals and, perhaps, insecurities that we nod in agreement but do nothing to spur on ourselves or those around us to bring these dreams to reality.

Jesus took the daily happenings of life and miraculously turned the world upside down.

He had the IT factor — He ignited transformation everywhere He went. When Peter was discouraged with his lack of fishing success, Jesus ignited transformation by encouraging Peter to take one more step of faith. Peter was convinced that there were no fish to be caught, let alone enough to break his net, but he obeyed (Luke 5:4–6).

You might think, *Yes, but that was Jesus. That was a miracle, and it's wrong to equate that supernatural event with everyday life.*

Peter experienced this transformational event in the midst of his everyday life. In the midst of a discouraging and unproductive day, he saw that the influence of a *transformation igniter* totally changed his perspective on the possibility that was right before him. If we have the Spirit of the Living God, the same Spirit that raised Jesus Christ from the grave, dwelling within us, why do we think that God can't use us to ignite transformation too? Remember that Jesus said that we would "do even greater things [works] than these" after He was resurrected (John 14:12).

When we know Jesus and are allowing Him to lead us, the IT factor is working within us this very moment. Our spirits have been transformed from death unto life because of the risen Savior we embrace. His forgiveness has ignited transformation in the depths of our very being, and we are called to pass it on.

Picture ten matches standing side by side, all in a row. One match ignites the one beside it, which ignites the next and so on until all are ablaze. Often when we are used to light a spiritual fire, we do not have a clue how far our flame will reach. We are not responsible for what the next match in our row does, but if we know that we have wisdom, compassion, or leadership burning within us, we are compelled to use what we have to help ignite a spiritual flame in others.

Recently while I was teaching and leading worship at a retreat, the dedicated director, Debbie, said, "Lisa, I understand the premise of igniting transformation, and I love the concept. However, there are women I've been investing in through numerous studies at church. They have an abundance of head knowledge, but they admit they struggle with trusting God."

I explained to her that we often run into similar situations as we teach believers. Some women who have been born-again for decades have spent the majority of their lives in secular environments — some call it "the real world" — where they may have no interaction with other believers. In such cases we need to consider that we may be attempting to light a wet match. Imagine that the match we're trying to light with another match has been sitting in a damp place for quite a while. It has not ceased being a match — it still has phosphorous on its stick, but if moisture has soaked into its fiber (think soul-dampening elements such as betrayal, abandonment, abuse, etc.), it's safe to assume that they will have had a negative effect.

After I gave the damp-match analogy, Debbie smiled and became encouraged that perhaps some of the women she was mentoring were "dehumidifying" through her consistent Spirit-led help.

We should embrace the IT factor with which we've been equipped to speak truth and encouragement into the precious eternal beings that God has called us to walk with throughout this life on earth. At times, our IT approach will be direct. Other times, it will be by parenting or mentoring or modeling behavior as God desires, based on His sovereign influence in our lives.

If you question whether or not you have the IT factor, then perhaps it's time to evaluate your life. Ask yourself: *Do I know where I'm going? Do I know beyond a shadow of a doubt that Jesus Christ lives in me by the indwelling of the Holy Spirit? Can I be an igniter for transformation in other's lives because I've witnessed it in my own life? Is there a fire burning within me that is catching? Does God use what I have to light up the lives, hopes, dreams, skills, and missions of those around me?*

Read John 15 and look, perhaps for the first time, at how important it is to abide in relationship with the only One who can truly ignite, facilitate, encourage, and reveal to you His personal transformational work that you've been called to ignite wherever He pleases.

HOW TO USE "THE IT FACTOR" SECTIONS

You can go through "The IT Factor" sections on your own, or you can meet weekly with a group and have a roundtable discussion. Based on our experience, we would recommend meeting with a group. Yes, that may seem a little scary, and I am sure you can think of many reasons to avoid it. But if you want to grow, if you want to encourage the development of others, if you want to ignite transformation, then you need to climb out of your comfort zone, commit to investing the time to develop the gifts God has given you, and learn to more fully realize His call on your life. Here's how to begin:

1. Meet once a week with a small group of people (three to eight) for one hour.
2. There are four sections to "The IT Factor": a descriptive portion, the Benefits of the Value, the Characteristics, and the Steps to Follow.
3. Take turns going around the table and reading "The IT Factor" aloud.
4. At the end of each section, there are one or two questions for the group to answer. Take a couple of minutes to discuss your answers before moving on to the next section.
5. The last portion of "The IT Factor" asks you to come up with a specific, measurable action step. Take a couple of minutes so

that group members can write down their action for the next week. Hint: Make the action step measurable by making sure you include a who, what, where, or when in it. For example: "I will use affirming words this week" would be too broad of a step and is not easily measured. Something like "I will use affirming words with people as I leave the office this week" is specific, easily measured, and sets you up for the best chance to succeed.

6. Each person then shares her action step with the group.
7. When you get together the next week, share the story of how you did with your action step and any positive effects you noticed because of it. Then start on the next "IT Factor."

So let's *do* IT — full of belief, confident that we're presentable inside and out. Let's keep a firm grip on the promises that keep us going. He always keeps His word. Let's see how inventive we can be in encouraging love and helping out, not avoiding worshipping together as some do but spurring each other on, especially as we "see the Day approaching" (Hebrews 10:22–25 *The Message*).

CHAPTER 1

THE VALUE OF UNDERSTANDING PEOPLE

The Proverbs 31 woman understood the simplicity of living out her eternal purpose day by day. Her understanding of people flowed through her household and into the marketplace. Because she understood her husband, he placed his confidence and trust in her judgment (v. 11) and she encouraged him to reach his greatest potential. Her understanding of people flowed through her household and into the marketplace as she gave counsel and instruction (v. 26).

One of the deepest desires of the human heart is to be understood. Our culture is full of voices crying out to be understood. Our entertainment — music, TV, movies, and even our Facebook status updates — reflect a deep desire to be understood.

Our life experience, personality, gifts, hopes, dreams, prejudices, and insecurities are all factors that form an equation that produces as many different answers as there are people drawing breath. How often have our past or present comments, if taken out of context, been appallingly misunderstood?

Even Jesus has been misunderstood. He has been misrepresented throughout the chronicles of history by humans who place our own, as Dr. Rick Warren says, *hurt, habits, and hang-ups* on our perception of Jesus, His message, His intentions, His lifestyle, and His deity.

The principle of understanding people reminds us of the four basic needs that dwell within every human heart: to be appreciated, to experience achievement, to have a sense of belonging, and to feel secure. If we, as marketplace leaders, teachers, facilitators, and family members fail to input some aspect of each of those needs into the lives of those in our realm of influence, we have failed to understand how to create an environment where we all win.

Are you longing for peace in your environment? Learn to understand those who are part of the landscape. Desire to influence those around you? Live in a way that makes them yearn to tap into their own God-given potential. Do you want to motivate others? Help them to visualize the potential fruit of their labor and understand the impact and value their efforts hold. You cannot succeed in those areas without understanding people.

The key to successful sales is understanding people. You can have the most incredible, time- and money-saving product or the best-tasting, most innovative food solution. If, however, you cannot connect with the consumer, you will be nothing but a fast-fading flare in the marketplace. Unfortunately, this is a common occurrence in the business world and prevents many from achieving the levels of success of which they are capable.

The truth is you can't give away what you don't have. My role as a leader is to learn, grow, and challenge myself to skillfully and intelligently develop. Understanding people has to be a key focus of that growth. If I can better understand people, and be better understood by them, that will create a foundation upon which to build a relationship. Once that relationship develops, I am given access to their heart.

Even when dealing with someone who is antagonistic to the person of Jesus (because no one is neutral, as some suggest), His influence in my life, His wisdom and compassion within me, spurs me on to show evidence of His presence in my attitude, creativity, and leadership.

I'm quick to admit that I've been stretched in ways I would have preferred to avoid: professionally, spiritually, emotionally, and physically. I've offended others. Mostly it has been unintentional, but sometimes it has come from pride, positional leadership, anger, hurt, or confusion.

I've found that understanding people as a corporate leader necessitates seeking God. As Dr. Henry Blackaby in his book *Experiencing God* encourages us, I am to "see where He is working and join Him there." Unfortunately, I've made the mistake in both the marketplace and ministry leadership of seeing where I want to work, and telling God to join me there.

— *Lisa*

A THIRSTY WOMAN

Jesus' skill at understanding people is perfect. He is God and omniscient, but His Spirit in us can be our inspiration for understanding others. John 16:13 states, "But when he, the Spirit of truth, comes, he will guide you into all truth. He will not speak on his own; he will speak only what he hears, and he will tell you what is yet to come."

In a perfect example of Jesus' people skills, John tells us that when Jesus left Judea and traveled to Galilee He "had to go through Samaria on the way" (John 4:4 NLT). The reason was not geographic but purposeful; He had to go that way to meet a woman at a well. Read

John 4:5–30 for the whole story of their interaction and the impact on the woman's life. It begins:

> *Eventually he came to the Samaritan village of Sychar, near the field that Jacob gave to his son Joseph. Jacob's well was there; and Jesus, tired from the long walk, sat wearily beside the well about noontime. Soon a Samaritan woman came to draw water, and Jesus said to her, "Please give me a drink." He was alone at the time because his disciples had gone into the village to buy some food.*
>
> *The woman was surprised, for Jews refuse to have anything to do with Samaritans. She said to Jesus, "You are a Jew, and I am a Samaritan woman. Why are you asking me for a drink?"*
>
> *Jesus replied, "If you only knew the gift God has for you and who you are speaking to, you would ask me, and I would give you living water"* (John 4:5–10 NLT).

Jesus chose to go through a region most Jews avoided and to speak with a woman they would have — at the very least — ignored. Both the woman and Jesus' disciples were surprised that He would talk to a Samaritan woman. Jesus chose their mutual need of water as a common denominator. He, a Jewish rabbi, and a Samaritan woman couldn't have been more different from the world's perspective. Jesus spoke with purpose to draw out her confession of circumstances (having had five husbands and currently living with another man), not for His sake, but hers. He spoke directly and simply so that He would be understood. He also must have communicated to her through tone of voice and posture that He was willing to listen to what she had to say, that He cared about her, even though He did not agree with her choices.

We can assume this woman felt misunderstood and that her sense of displacement socially and spiritually led her to a solitary, lonely existence. By coming to the well midday, she would likely be avoiding others who came in the cooler morning or evening hours. The Samaritan woman was intelligent, as demonstrated by her dialogue with Jesus. He met her where there was need (physical, spiritual, and emotional) and spoke to her about "living water" (v. 10). Why? Because she could grasp the concept of that need in her life. She was coming to the well with a bucket in her hand!

We are often at our most effective with others when we choose to encounter them on their own turf. Jesus knew that it was the right place, at the right time. Purposefulness and wisdom in choosing our encounters are necessary elements in understanding others.

Our influence will have ever-increasing impact on those around us when we develop the skill of speaking so others hear and understand what we are saying. We also need to learn the skill of intentional listening, which can be defined as hearing beyond the words that are being said (without inappropriate speculation). When we consider where people are coming from — their background and life circumstances — and try to be sensitive to their emotional state, we have a better chance of communicating well.

> "Knowing what people need and want is the key to understanding them. And if you can understand them, you can influence them in a positive way."
> — *Winning with People*, Dr. John C. Maxwell

One of the greatest qualities you can possess is to learn to understand people. In order to do this, you must use every resource within you.

Here are four key elements in learning to understand people: listen intently, collect and process facts, learn to read a person's body language, and cultivate empathy. The neglect of any one of these four elements results in ineffective communication. Poor communication stunts growth, ushers in division and confusion, minimizes productivity, and results in emotionally anorexic relationships. An emotionally malnourished relationship is one where there is no possibility for growth.

LISTEN INTENTLY

Discipline involves the elimination of distractions. In our high-tech world, this is a challenge for all of us. As part of a society which prides itself in the ability to reach anyone, anywhere, at any time, the skill of listening intently requires a purposeful removal of our attention from many other demands. The redirection of our attention solely on the one whom we wish to understand says, before anything else is said, that we believe there is value in what they are about to share. This provides a forum for a more full expression of their thoughts and feelings.

To let people know that you hear them, you must look them in the eye. Maintaining eye contact is a way to show both respect and interest. When we don't look people in the eyes, we may create distrust within them. Societal norms dictate that a lack of eye contact indicates a disinterest or lack of integrity. One of the most frequent complaints of baby boomers, or anyone over the age of 30, is that it can't be known if the person whose face is in their smartphone is actually hearing what is being said.

A third indication that you are listening is repeating back what you have heard. Repeating verbatim either in a statement or in the form of a question can be beneficial. Begin with "I heard you say," and then repeat word for word what you heard the other person say. If you were to begin this same interaction instead with "you said," you would potentially set up a volatile situation where the person feels accused rather than heard. This creates an emotional disconnect that not only impedes the progression of communication but also potentially discredits prior positive interactions. You could lose any ground you gained.

One of the most challenging things is to make sure people feel truly heard. I have a multitasking mind-set; there are always several things going on at once. Setting everything aside to show people they matter enough to be listened to is both difficult and extremely valuable. I have had to discipline myself to focus on others when it is time to listen.

One practical thing I have done is to position my computer facing the wall rather than facing the people who sit across from me in my office. This reminds me to turn around and look at them when they talk and prevents me from being distracted by email or things on which I was working. Another thing that has helped me is to turn off the ringer on my phone and shut off other electronic devices when there is something important being discussed. I also try to make notes of what people say so that I can both remember what they talked about and show them that what they say is important to me.

Perhaps the most difficult and yet important place to show I am intently listening is at home with my husband and our kids. For me, this requires intentionality and focus. If the most valuable people in my life feel unimportant because they do not feel heard, my world begins to unravel. To set myself up for success, I internally make appointments with them to listen. For example, when I pick the kids up from school, that is listening time. I do all I can to stay off my phone so that I can gauge their mood, ask them questions about their day, and have an opportunity to connect. With my husband, our time to connect is usually later in the evening after the kids have gone to bed. We are both night owls, so this is the time that works best for us. When I do well as a listener, everyone seems to get along better.

— *Dawn*

COLLECT AND PROCESS FACTS

Some people are all feelings and no facts. The truth is, there are factual facts and emotional facts, and both are needed to arrive at an accurate conclusion. Trial attorneys can present a plethora of circumstantial evidence and with theatrical persuasion bring about the outcome they desire. It is a mark of wisdom to be able to separate facts from feelings. Some personalities have an instinctual ability to be more descriptive about situations, causing some to be more believable than others. This is important to be aware of when in a position of leadership.

Getting the facts encompasses the basics: who, what, where, why, and how? Just as there are some who are more persuasive in their presentation, others must be encouraged in order to get to the heart of the matter. We must be diligent to get both sides of the story.

If we are only partially engaged in a conversation, we will miss significant details. Just as we need to collect the facts, we need to listen to the emotions, otherwise we only get part of the picture. So much of what is said goes beyond the realm of words. (This is one reason emails are often misunderstood.) Because we are all emotional beings, when the emotional aspect is neglected, people are left with a sense of not being fully understood.

Listening, without collecting all the facts, potentially enables someone to feel justified in continuing to make poor choices or give bad advice. If they think you don't understand, your opinion has little value. Acknowledging and affirming that you recognize their position is the first brick in building the wall of trust.

READ BODY LANGUAGE

Body language is nonverbal communication. It is either the invitation to or the resistance of interpersonal acceptance. Some experts assert that approximately 90 percent of human communication consists of body language cues which indicate the attitude or state of mind of a person. Being attentive to body language offers a gauge with which we can determine the level of emotional openness. A person's body language may convey feelings such as openness, happiness, disappointment, anger, withdrawal, resentment, shame, and mistrust. It is important to be aware of the messages others are sending as well as the messages we send in our interactions.

DEVELOP EMPATHY

Another aspect of understanding people well requires setting aside preconceived ideas, assumptions, or conclusions so that we are able to experience people as they truly are, rather than through our own emotional and circumstantial filters. Often people can remind us of someone else we know and we may begin to judge them subconsciously, projecting negative vibes that did not originate with or belong to them. When this happens, we can start to categorize, trust, or dismiss them based on the memories or feelings they bring to the surface. This hinders the ability of new, healthy, or positive relationship ties to be established.

Some of us are probably thinking, "Yes, that has happened to me, and I am usually right." God has given many of us the gift of discernment, and certainly there are some who read people very well. But no one is *always* right. This is especially important when we are seen as the authority in a situation. Whether we are someone's mom, teacher, or leader, we have accepted a varying degree of responsibility for that person's development. An incorrect assumption can put a person into a box he or she can never climb out of. We also can become hypervigilant looking for proof of our false assumptions to validate our estimation. If we do not give each person the opportunity to be known before we decide who and what they are, we may be missing out on an amazing gift or learning experience God intends for us or for them.

A person should be trusted until they present a reason to not be. Although we can and should be cautious if we feel uncomfortable with someone, we cannot solely rely on our emotions to determine our assessment. If we can avoid being swayed by our own assumptions and expectations, we can begin to get a grasp on where the other person is really coming from. We may begin to see why they do what they do and why they are the way they are. This will alter our perception and give their responses a whole new meaning.

Solomon, the wisest man in the world (1 Kings 3:12), was given amazing insight and ability to understand people. His proverbs talk about all kinds of people — the lazy, the mockers, the righteous and reverent, and finally the ambitious and successful. His observations recorded in Scripture show that he understood all types of people and how best to relate to them.

First Kings 3:16–28 relates the story of two prostitutes who came to King Solomon with a problem. They lived in the same house and had both recently given birth to baby boys. One of them claimed that the other had stolen her son (she had exchanged the children when she rolled over in bed on her baby and he died). Whose baby was the surviving child? They argued before the king, neither of them willing to give ground. Solomon showed the value of knowing others — their background, their needs and their possible motivations. When he suggested they divide the baby in half, one woman agreed, but the real mother immediately begged for the child to remain living — even if it meant he would go to the other woman. This ability to understand others brought Solomon success, great fame, and respect from those around them. "When all Israel heard the king's decision, the people were in awe of the king, for they saw the wisdom God had given him for rendering justice" (1 Kings 3:28 NLT).

The value of understanding people affects every area of our lives — our families, our work, our friends, and especially our enemies or those with whom we have conflict. When we endeavor to understand others we show them we care, effectively obeying two mandates — to love others (John 13:34) and to love our enemies (Luke 6:27) — given to us in Scripture. When others know we care, it can change the way they perceive us, the way they listen to us and how they respond to us. This, in turn, can give us opportunity to positively impact and influence them. The simple fact is, as someone has said, people don't care how much you know until they know how much you care.

BECOME AN UNDERSTANDING LEADER

From a leadership standpoint, it is important to understand people so we can motivate and serve them, encouraging creativity and productivity in our workplaces. This gives us a tremendous advantage in team building. When we understand people, we are better able to identify their strengths and weaknesses and place them where they will most often operate in their area of strength. In doing this, we show them that we recognize them as individuals while also giving them the opportunity to be a part of something great. This builds morale for the entire team as each person is set up to succeed both as individuals and as a team. People need to know that our heart is for them.

Recognizing another's point of view (even if we don't agree with them) shows respect for their unique God-given qualities. We are more alike than different, and endeavoring to understand others helps us recognize and reinforce our commonalities. This also creates a grace-filled atmosphere in which we cultivate a forgiving attitude toward others as we admit our own mistakes.

One of the most challenging aspects of the principle of understanding people is that we are too often self-focused. It takes practice and discipline to listen for meaning and understanding of what is being said and focus on the other person's words rather than thinking about and planning what we are going to say in return. This involves paying close attention to what the other person is saying and how they are feeling, rather than one's own reaction. Committing to try to see things from a different perspective than our own opens the lines of communication and allows thoughts, ideas, and feelings to flow freely. Considering another's emotional response can help us to change not only our outlook, but theirs as well.

The benefits of developing the skill of understanding people spills over into our family relationships as well. Our relationships with our spouses, children, and extended family are dramatically impacted by the amount of care we put into understanding each person.

Between the two of us (Dawn and Lisa), we have been blessed with six children. Each of them is unique in personality, communication style, energy level, and perception of self. We must meet our children where they are in their development and personality rather than where we would like for them to be or where their brother or sister was at that age.

We have both been married for over 20 years. Some have the misconception that women who are strong leaders are lacking in the area of godly submission within the home. However, our husbands encourage us to be all that God designed us to be. For this we are truly thankful.

Many women might be surprised to find that each of us willingly stated in our wedding vows that we would obey our husband. We acknowledge that not every marriage shares the same relational dynamics that ours do. Making an effort to understand your spouse, however, can make a world of difference. You should not be making more of an effort to understand others than you are to understand your own spouse. We have each found that the implementation of this truth has been essential to enjoying a strong and healthy marriage.

SHARPEN YOUR UNDERSTANDING

So how do we implement this value of understanding others into our lives? More wisdom from Proverbs 27:17 (NLT) says, "As iron sharpens iron, so a friend sharpens a friend." Learning about this principle is not enough. We need to take steps of action to make it a part of our lives in order to become powerful influencers in the lives of others. By inviting others to join you in discussing this principle, you will learn from each other, effectively *sharpening* each other and helping each other develop this attribute.

We encourage using an effective method called a "roundtable," which creates a learning environment that allows everyone to meet on neutral ground or peer to peer. Encouraging each person around the table to participate in the discussion fosters an atmosphere of learning and growth as each individual chooses an area of their life to work on in the coming week, returning the following week to express their success, or struggle, in these areas. Reflecting on the principle of the week, then responding to a short self-evaluation helps each person recognize the next steps they need to take.

The goal in understanding people is never to manipulate them but to better relate to them, to motivate them, to forgive them, and to work together with them. Understanding people is a spiritual discipline that will change our lives and impact the people around us for God's eternal glory.

THE IT FACTOR

■ UNDERSTANDING PEOPLE

The purposes of a person's heart are deep waters, but one who has insight draws them out.

— Proverbs 20:5

Understanding people requires listening from your heart while using your head.

- When we understand why people do what they do and why they are the way they are, we will be able to better relate to them, motivate them, forgive them, and work with them.

- The ability to understand people affects every area of your life — family, work, and friends — because it involves communication with others.

- It involves setting aside your preconceived ideas and assumptions in order to experience people as they really are rather than who they remind you of or what you would like for them to be.

- Making an effort to understand others is a way to show them that you care and will often change the way they feel about you. It gives you an opportunity to be Jesus to someone else. Showing others understanding and compassion will give you opportunities to positively influence and impact them.
- Every person has at least four basic needs: to be appreciated, to experience a sense of achievement, to have a sense of belonging, and to feel secure. We should keep these in mind in all our dealings with people.
- When we understand people, we create a positive environment in which people feel heard and encouraged and their needs are met.

■ QUESTION

Do you intentionally make an effort to understand others? Are you ever tempted to judge people before you really know them?

■ BENEFITS OF UNDERSTANDING PEOPLE

If you are a person who understands people, you will experience the following benefits:

- You will strengthen the relationships with the people who matter most to you.
- God will use you as a person of influence. You will have the opportunity to encourage and motivate others and to affect them positively. People will want to spend time with you.
- You will be able to communicate effectively with others. This will save you from a lot of unnecessary conflict and bring more peace to your environment.
- You will see the potential in others and contribute to helping them develop it.

- You will recognize people's strengths and weaknesses. This will help you to build a strong team that capitalizes on everyone's strengths.

■ CHARACTERISTICS OF UNDERSTANDING PEOPLE

People who are good at understanding people:

- Make an effort to see things from another's point of view.
- Recognize and respect everyone's unique qualities. They have a good grasp on the meaning of 1 Corinthians 12 where Paul describes the benefits and variety of the giftedness God gives:

> God's various gifts are handed out everywhere; but they all originate in God's Spirit. God's various ministries are carried out everywhere; but they all originate in God's Spirit. God's various expressions of power are in action everywhere; but God himself is behind it all. Each person is given something to do that shows who God is: Everyone gets in on it, everyone benefits (1 Corinthians 12:4–7 *The Message*).

- Realize that people have a lot in common and reinforce that to create a team atmosphere.
- Are good listeners and ask questions to clarify when they are unsure.
- Have a forgiving attitude because they understand there are reasons behind what people do. This understanding enables them to more easily forgive others' mistakes or indiscretions.

■ QUESTION

Do you know someone who demonstrates an ability to understand people? What do you admire about that person? What must you do to be more like him or her?

■ UNDERSTANDING PEOPLE: STEPS TO FOLLOW

Develop a specific measurable action step to take this week by:

1. **Focusing on the other person.** Really listening to someone takes more than just hearing their words. When you listen intently, you are looking for the meaning in their words, paying attention to their body language and focusing on their facial expressions. You have to *feel* them as well as hear them.

2. **Not listening in order to reply; listen to understand.** The biggest mistake you can make when communicating with others is to put your focus on what *you* want to say and how *you* feel about something. Instead, you need to stop yourself from planning your next sentence and listen very closely to what *the other person* is saying and how *he or she is* feeling.

3. **Looking at situations from the other person's point of view.** Step outside yourself and look at things from their perspective. Ask God to help you see and have empathy for what they are experiencing.

4. **Considering the effects of emotions on a situation.** Keep in mind that everyone has an emotional reaction to the things that are happening around them. Often these emotions could be rooted in what is going on in their life rather than the actual situation at hand. When conflicts arise, do all you can to get to the heart of the matter before you allow yourself to react to the emotional outburst that is occurring.

5. **Recognizing and respecting the unique qualities of those in your environment.** Remember that every person has the desire and need to be valued and appreciated.

> *The beginning of wisdom is this: Get wisdom. Though it cost all you have, get understanding.*
>
> — Proverbs 4:7

CHAPTER 2

THE VALUE OF FORGIVENESS

How do we know that forgiveness was an essential attribute of the Proverbs 31 woman's character? Because of the reaction of her husband and children: "Her children arise and call her blessed; her husband also, and he praises her" (Proverbs 31:28). Every wife and mother experiences plenty of slights and wrongs in her family life, deliberate or not, that necessitate forgiveness. The emotionally closed-off or vindictive woman who can never forgive and get past wrongs (real or perceived) done against her may still be loved by her family. But they won't be jumping to their feet to loudly attest to how blessed they were to have her. Instead, she will be the object of whispered conversations such as, "Well, you know that's just how Mom is."

Forgiveness. It is often the most treasured outcome for the forgiven and the most challenging effort for the forgiver. While forgiveness is sometimes seen as a religious ritual full of piety or even an unguaranteed emotional "put it behind you" tranquilizer, it is neither a one-time act nor a blanket brushing away of consequences and offense. Forgiveness must be based on truth. True forgiveness is an act of the will that is implemented in the depths of our spirit — sometimes daily, hourly, or even moment by moment, depending on the offense.

Women (and men) who would be leaders in the real world must have a lifestyle of forgiveness. Without it, we are guaranteed to become obsessive, embittered, and mistrusting. Holding on to grudges in any area of life can affect our decisions and attitudes toward those we lead and hope to influence. In examining Jesus and His approach to life and relationships, we will find He was consistently full of *both* grace and truth.

In the world's cutthroat mentality toward business, a marketplace environment where grace and truth abound may seem out of place. However, belonging, growth, and productivity are all part of the natural resources we as Christ-following leaders need to share and cultivate. Utilizing these vital resources is impossible outside of the principle of forgiveness being exercised — purposefully, strategically, and habitually.

In our Christ-given mandate we are instructed to forgive as we have been forgiven (Matthew 6:14–15; Luke 6:37). The story Jesus gives us in Matthew 18:21–35 (*The Message*) perfectly illustrates the need to offer to others the forgiveness Christ freely offers to us:

> At that point Peter got up the nerve to ask, "Master, how many times do I forgive a brother or sister who hurts me? Seven?"
>
> Jesus replied, "Seven! Hardly. Try seventy times seven.
>
> "The kingdom of God is like a king who decided to square accounts with his servants. As he got under way, one servant was brought before him who had run up a debt of a hundred thousand dollars. He couldn't pay up, so the king ordered the man, along with his wife, children, and goods, to be auctioned off at the slave market.
>
> "The poor wretch threw himself at the king's feet and begged, 'Give me a chance and I'll pay it all back.' Touched by his plea, the king let him off, erasing the debt.

"The servant was no sooner out of the room when he came upon one of his fellow servants who owed him ten dollars. He seized him by the throat and demanded, 'Pay up. Now!'

"The poor wretch threw himself down and begged, 'Give me a chance and I'll pay it all back.' But he wouldn't do it. He had him arrested and put in jail until the debt was paid. When the other servants saw this going on, they were outraged and brought a detailed report to the king.

"The king summoned the man and said, 'You evil servant! I forgave your entire debt when you begged me for mercy. Shouldn't you be compelled to be merciful to your fellow servant who asked for mercy?' The king was furious and put the screws to the man until he paid back his entire debt. And that's exactly what my Father in heaven is going to do to each one of you who doesn't forgive unconditionally anyone who asks for mercy."

Many deceive themselves by believing because they are passive, nonconfrontational, or outwardly resigned to troubling situations, that they are forgiving. That's incorrect! (This reaction can actually be a type of passive aggression.) Forgiveness is an intentional release of a debt owed — it is an act of the heart. Releasing situations, people, disappointments, betrayals, and ourselves to God and believing, because He has all the facts, that He is the best one to go to when we need to extend or receive forgiveness is what Jesus taught us and showed us. The sacrificial leadership that took Jesus to Calvary is the same style of leadership that forgives mistakes, both intentional and accidental, and focuses on healthy restoration.

Our forgiveness of others releases us to become all God intended us to be without the baggage of bitterness or unforgiveness. It also releases the offender into the hands of God — tough and tender — to do just as He wills. The act of forgiveness is key in moving us forward as an individual, couple, family, corporate team, or church body.

No living thing can thrive with the disease of unforgiveness destroying everything healthy in its environment. It's like putting cyanide in your office water cooler. Maybe no one sees or tastes it, but its life-destroying poison will impact everyone exposed to the treacherous mixture.

WORKPLACE FORGIVENESS

There are many opportunities to forgive in the workplace. One of the biggest drivers of this is just the amount of time we spend at work. If you are spending eight hours a day or more at work, you are probably spending more of your waking hours with your workmates than you do with family and friends. Often, these are people that you did not choose — you just ended up on the same team. Yet you need to find ways to work together. Add to that the fact that work environments are often comprised of high-pressure situations like meeting deadlines, achieving metrics and goals, profit and loss considerations, and problem solving, and it starts to become obvious why practicing forgiveness at work is necessary. Pressure reveals character. Put enough pressure on someone, and you will begin to see the chinks in their armor. That goes for everyone because we all have areas that could be improved upon when it comes to character.

When you grow up in a family business, as I did, it is like growing up on a farm. For instance, if you grew up on a dairy farm, you learned how to milk cows. Whatever business you grow up in, you learn how to do what your family does. Even as a child, I had "chores" to do in the business. They were comprised of anything I was physically able to do or assist anyone else in doing. That translates to: Dad had us try it all.

The summer I was 13 years old, I worked in the darkroom. My job was to make photos a certain size so they would fit on the advertisement we were putting together for a magazine. The lady I worked for would give me the sizes I was to shoot. Then I would give them back, and she would put the ads together. Sounds simple enough. The problem was she would give me incorrect sizes sometimes and, instead of admitting a mistake, she would blame me. I didn't get in trouble for it, and the problem could be corrected. But it resulted in some wasted time doing it over, and I was bothered that she blamed me. The first few times, I thought maybe she didn't realize she had made the mistake. Then I started to believe she knew it was her mistake, but I was an easy scapegoat because I was a kid. I began harboring some angry, unforgiving feelings toward her. I spent that summer looking for ways to prove she was wrong and being unhappy in my job.

Eventually, I figured out that it wasn't worth it to hold on to a grudge. All it did was make my hours at work drag on and make me feel worse. I would even dwell on it after I went home. Thirty years later, I still remember that summer and how mad I was. I imagine the lady who was giving me orders doesn't remember. My attitude didn't make her miserable; it made me miserable. That is the first time I learned that it's better to let the bitterness go and forgive as quickly as you can.

Another reason it can be hard to forgive on the job is because we work with people we have invested in and trusted. When that trust is broken, it can be extremely hurtful and disappointing. I have run into this many times over the years. As a young adult, I watched people at work take advantage of my parents' generosity. I got so upset with them that it was difficult for me not to be suspect of everyone. Isn't that how it works? You experience a breach of trust, and it begins to color your other interactions. It is good to be discerning and to expect others to earn your trust. However, it is crippling to constantly be suspicious, always looking for the worst-case scenario.

This crippling scenario is created by a combination of unforgiveness and pride. We are unable to forgive the betrayals of others and are too proud to give someone else a chance or the benefit of the doubt. That old saying, "Fool me once, shame on you. Fool me twice, shame on me," is pride taking hold of our psyche. I know because I have said it. The feeling that drove me to make that remark was my pride not allowing that I could make a mistake in my estimation of someone.

If you have invested in someone's development, it can be even worse. There once was a manager I had had spent a lot of time developing because I could see great potential. The problem was this person would take one step forward and two steps back — make a good leadership call followed by an inappropriate comment or scathing email. Time after time, I would listen, counsel, and try to help repair damaged work relationships. Just when I thought things were getting better, the person would make another poor decision. It culminated in this person doing something so inappropriate at work that termination was the only answer. I felt betrayed. I had stuck my neck out, spent countless hours in listening, training, and development, only to have the whole thing blow up in my face. This time, however, I chose to forgive right away. I was sad and disappointed about how things had turned out, but I had learned that carrying a grudge was not worth the personal cost that comes with unforgiveness.

How do you forgive people at work? You make the choice to let it go (whether the offending party is still employed there or not). It isn't based on your feelings or your rights. When the thought comes up, you choose to focus on something else. If someone wants to start a conversation about it, you turn the conversation to another subject. You spend your time on what you can change, rather than on what you can't. And you depend on the grace of God to be able to forgive, just as you must in other areas of your life.

HOW TO RISE UP AND FORGIVE

Have you run across someone in your office who is judgmental and unforgiving? Most likely that wasn't just a random character trait. I find that those who are the most judgmental have learned from a mentor or an abusive situation. Perhaps a parent attempted to live vicariously through a child who didn't possess the natural talent that was a priority to the mom or dad. Criticism of the child was constant, and a judgmental spirit was unconsciously passed on. Or a mistrusting spirit could have been cultivated through years of abuse and/or neglect. The child couldn't trust the parent — or anyone else in the future.

It's a tough role to play — exhausting, in fact — for those who walk in unforgiveness have the incredible pressure of having to be right all the time. Their pride will destroy any opportunity to acknowledge that they might, just might, not be completely correct in their perspective.

In leadership, unforgiveness is a guaranteed defeat or loss for your team. As seeds of anger, insecurity, mistrust, and condemnation grow, the inevitable harvest will destroy creativity and unity. If there is an unforgiving person in your company, please wisely develop a two-prong plan. Pray for them, exhibit forgiveness to them — but do not expose other employees or co-workers to them to whatever degree that is possible. And sadly, if you sense a hardness and bitterness that they seem unwilling to release, then wisely and strategically develop a plan either to lessen their interaction and influence with others. Or find an appropriate approach to remove them from the organization. (The time frame requires prayer and wisdom from God.)

When you cannot avoid the poison that a personality injects into an environment, you need to walk in forgiveness. But you are also responsible to protect your organization's employees and reputation. Hebrews 12:15 warns about the bitter root that can ruin everything or spoil the whole garden. There is no deeper or more destructive root than the one of bitterness. Please bear in mind, there are most certainly consequences for ill-conceived approaches in the marketplace, but there are times when your survival will depend on your ability to forgive a co-worker for a deep and cutting offense.

— *Lisa*

Someone with an unforgiving spirit will continually try to quell or denigrate the gifts and talents of the one who is its object, not wanting the object of distain to achieve any level of success. That attitude looks at each attribute of the unforgiven person through the clouded lens of contempt.

For business, it all seems so personal, you may say. It is! For us to have marketplace environments where grace and truth abound, belonging, growth, and productivity have to be part of the natural resources leaders share and cultivate. But these crucial elements to success are impossible to achieve outside of the principle of forgiveness being exercised strategically and habitually.

There's no guarantee of anyone else's forgiveness, but God's is guaranteed when we say to Him, "I was wrong, please forgive me." Once we receive His forgiveness, it's a done deal. We're told that if we "confess our sins, [God] is faithful and just to forgive us our sins and purify us from all unrighteousness" (1 John 1:9). Notice that it talks about confessing "our sins." We are not responsible for another's response.

Whether in the marketplace, at home, or in the church, when we are recognizing and implementing the value of forgiveness, God and His Son, Jesus Christ are glorified. Without practicing forgiveness, we cannot be a Spirit-led Christian. How often have we heard, "I was at church every time the doors were open. My parents made sure of that. I still believe, but I don't practice organized religion anymore!"? Due to the fact that some are so *committed* to being *uncommitted*, you gain the impression that forgiving some negative experiences from church days became a much larger challenge than turning away from the One who died to forgive them.

FORGIVING THE SEEMINGLY UNFORGIVEABLE

If there's a woman who would be justified in the eyes of the world if she were bitter, angry and unforgiving, it would be Becki Reiser. She and her husband, Jeff, are seasoned believers. Devoted to the truth of God's Word and His work in our community, they are quick to serve. It's no surprise that Becki has been a devoted wife and mom, school and church secretary, and a volunteer at Circle of Friends, a community outreach group that we (the authors) have been involved in for over a decade.

One of Becki's gifts is writing. She's written a manuscript, which we assume will soon be published. Its working title is *Through My*

Tears. What tears, you may ask? Becki has shed rivers of tears due to the evil perpetrated on her 17-year-old daughter, Liz. A happy, enthusiastic, God-following young woman, Liz was brutally assaulted by a man pretending to be in need of roadside assistance. Liz and her best friend were on their way home from a video rental store and, although Liz hesitated to pick up the man due to parental instruction, Brandy thought it was the compassionate response to a stranger in need.

What happened next is the ultimate nightmare for a parent. Brandy was devastated by the brutality that she survived at the hands of their assailant. Liz, on the other hand, was unable to testify about those events. She was found murdered soon after Brandy was discovered by authorities.

———

Another friend's son was murdered while listening to the horrible story of an abused woman co-worker who was attempting to flee her husband. A wrong place at the wrong time scenario placed Dianne Collard's son in the malicious path of a man who later confessed to the murder of the Collards' son.

So much promise, so much passion for God, so much life ahead. A young life blotted out!

———

How do we forgive the unforgiveable? Wouldn't a just God allow that Becki and Dianne, and other parents like them, were entitled to hate the monsters that took the lives of their children? And what about other murderers, pedophiles, pimps, and drug dealers, who disrespect the laws of God and man and bring tragedy into our homes? Are we supposed to forgive them?

Amazingly, both Becki and Dianne have used their respective and unique stories to share a common and much-needed message about forgiveness. Their stories are horrific and dramatic, but the act of forgiveness doesn't have to be connected with something as tragic as murder. We often learn more about forgiveness when we view it based on our own past, present, and future mistakes and sins — ones that we have committed or will inevitably commit. Throughout our lives, we each make choices that hurt God, others, and ourselves.

Is it wrong for a parent, spouse, or child to hang on to the hurt of an incredibly deep wound? We know that God expects us to forgive even when it seems unreasonable or impossible. His expectation is not unreasonable because He did it first by extending His forgiveness to us, the sin-stained perpetrators of His only Son's execution. Jesus Christ, who had no sin, became sin for us on the Cross (2 Corinthians 5:21). What caused Him to make that sacrifice? Go look in the mirror while I do the same.

A FALLEN WOMAN

Let's look at how Jesus dealt with someone whose lifestyle was such that she would have no reason to expect forgiveness — the woman caught in adultery (John 8:1–11 *The Message*):

> *Jesus went across to Mount Olives, but he was soon back in the Temple again. Swarms of people came to him. He sat down and taught them.*
>
> *The religion scholars and Pharisees led in a woman who had been caught in an act of adultery. They stood her in plain sight of everyone and said, "Teacher, this woman was caught red-handed in the act of adultery. Moses, in the Law, gives orders to stone such persons. What do you say?" They were trying to trap him into saying something*

incriminating so they could bring charges against him.

Jesus bent down and wrote with his finger in the dirt. They kept at him, badgering him. He straightened up and said, "The sinless one among you, go first: Throw the stone." Bending down again, he wrote some more in the dirt. Hearing that, they walked away, one after another, beginning with the oldest. The woman was left alone. Jesus stood up and spoke to her. "Woman, where are they? Does no one condemn you?"

"No one, Master."

"Neither do I," said Jesus. "Go on your way. From now on, don't sin."

For a moment think about that dusty, hot Middle Eastern day. Suddenly, a woman is thrust before Jesus as he taught in the Temple. A sinful woman caught in the act of adultery and dragged into the place appointed to worship God, a place of holiness and respect. Her sin was exposed before the religious crowd in town.

Can't you hear the gasps? The whispers?

Those in the woman's community had found a weapon to use against her, as well as Jesus. She couldn't escape the reality of her choices. However, Jesus equalized the battleground with His challenge to "the sinless one among you, go first: Throw the stone."

And then hear the stones they had picked up dropping one by one as the accusers all walk away and leave the woman alone with Jesus. This is high drama in any society.

With the unrighteous motives of the crowd revealed, Jesus addressed this woman's need for forgiveness. He assured her that there was pardon, not condemnation, available. But He was very specific when He told her to go and sin no more.

Amazing story, isn't it? A woman thrown in front of the Son of God. Not your everyday occurrence . . . or is it? Each and every day we all do things that bring a twinge or a typhoon of pain to the heart of God. We are all fallen creatures awaiting a time when all will be restored to what God originally intended. He's perfect, we're not, and no matter what has been done to us — or what we've done to others — forgiveness is the key to each of us finding peace with God. We receive God the Father's forgiveness through His One and only Son, Jesus Christ, and His completed work of redemption on Calvary.

Because of Jesus, we are not condemned. Because of Jesus, we are able to take our desire for restitution and our appetite for retribution toward others, and place them in the hand of God, who is great, good, and trustworthy. The imperfection of this world cries out for the power and reformation of forgiveness.

At peace with what is behind you and a genuine hope for the future that is before you. That is the gift of forgiveness.

We've read how Becki and Dianne have taken the brutal and unthinkable deaths of their children and offered their pain to God. I believe that sometimes the misperception is that because they've forgiven the murderers of their loved ones and juries have found them guilty, they no longer suffer pain. I think that's an unfortunate and false assumption. Each of them still have pain, but because they have been able to forgive, they have found the peace of God that passes all understanding.

HER FATHER'S DAUGHTER

How does an adult who was brutalized sexually, emotionally, or physically as a child take all the little-kid feelings and forgive as an adult?

The depth of pain or abuse suffered often determines the amount of time, trust, and truth required to bring that full release of forgiveness. Because forgiveness is a constant directive from God, those who rebel against it may eventually be so weary from carrying the load that their brokenness will overtake them. This brokenness will either lead them to a life far more abundant than any they could have dreamed of, or it will lead them to live like they have a rat gnawing and scratching on the recesses of their hearts. Those who allow God to *extract the rat* often have an incredible story of how even the most injured soul can become an incredible trophy of God's grace. Tanya is such a person.

Both of Tanya's parents were addicted to drugs and alcohol. She had no recollection of her father who was her first abuser, but she remembers all too well her grandfather who was her last. He killed himself ten days after she, at 15, reported that he had been molesting her for five years. He had always told her that, if she ever told anyone about the abuse, he would die and it would be all her fault. So even in death, he hurt her.

Besides her grandfather there were five other men who sexually abused her in her childhood. Men who had been invited into her life by her drug-addicted mother, men who left their mark on both of them. Somehow Tanya and her mother managed to function with the child in the role of her mother's caretaker and confidant. Tanya also became quite sufficient at taking care of herself. The gifts that characterize childhood such as innocence, purity, and irresponsibility were never hers to possess.

At 9 years old, Tanya and her mother came out of their last abusive situation together. They had been imprisoned for a year in a hotel room by a man that they were both deathly afraid of, and they suffered all types of abuse at his hands.

After they were finally freed, Tanya's mother had a complete breakdown. With nowhere else to turn, Tanya was abandoned to her grandfather and his wife. (Her mother had been estranged from her parents because it was her own father who had molested her when she was a child.)

Two months after Tanya revealed her grandfather's molestation, her mother married her fourth husband and moved out of the country. When Tanya's mother found out what had happened to her daughter, she blamed Tanya for not being "more careful" because she had warned her that her grandfather was dangerous.

The remainder of Tanya's growing-up years were also difficult. The abuse that she had endured for so many years finally began to take a toll on her. She struggled with severe depression, self-mutilation, and bulimia. She was hospitalized for repeated suicide attempts. Consumed with pain, inner loathing, and loneliness, she just wanted it all to stop.

Tanya's mother maintained a strained and difficult long-distance relationship with her. As much as Tanya longed for her mother to love her, she also began to hate her for all that she had failed to protect her from — all that she had never been for her. When Tanya was 16, her mother had a second child, a girl. This was the ultimate betrayal. Not only had Tanya been rejected and abandoned, suddenly she felt she had also been *replaced*. The root of bitterness within her heart toward her mother grew.

Tanya managed to graduate from high school and began college. At 19, she married a man who had no idea how much baggage she carried and how long the journey of healing would be. Healthy communication, trust, and intimacy were three necessities of marriage she knew nothing about, but her husband stood beside her with a patient and enduring love even in the most difficult times.

They eventually had two beautiful children even though doctors had predicted she couldn't have children because of the scars inflicted by her abusers.

After her conversion, the Lord restored so many areas in Tanya's life that she was convinced one day He would heal the relationship with her mother. Sadly, in 2008, Tanya's mother died from a drug overdose. She never was able to receive the restoration and redemption that the Lord had for her. At this point Tanya was a godly woman who loved the Lord with her whole heart and served Him as best as she could. However, because she had never been able to forgive her mother, the root of bitterness, unforgiveness, and even hatred remained in her heart. Death was just one more abandonment — the final abandonment.

Tanya's 14-year-old sister called to tell her that their mother had passed away. Tanya had purposefully never had a relationship with her sister because of the abandonment by her mother that she represented. That day Tanya told her that she was sorry but she wasn't coming to the funeral. Days later she made it clear to her sister's father that she wasn't interested in having a relationship with her sister.

A few months after her mother's death, Tanya began My Father's Daughter Ministries, and the Lord provided her opportunities to speak healing and truth into the lives of women. (Isn't God faithful to use us even while we're still in our own process of healing and restoration?)

Through life-giving truth offered to her in relationship with her Circle of Friends, she was lovingly confronted with the hatred and unforgiveness which remained locked away in her heart. Tanya was encouraged to seek Christian counseling and take steps to deal with those issues which had prevented her from walking in the fullness of freedom that Christ offers. Her Circle of Friends helped her understand that she was limping, not running, the race set before her and that — until she was willing to face what she had not faced and forgive — she would never be able to experience all that the Lord had for her.

Nothing about Tanya's process of healing was easy. There were days when her heart hurt so much that she didn't think she could move forward one more step. But, with the love and support of her husband and her Circle of Friends, she was able to face, accept, and grieve the loss of the mother she never really had. She was able to forgive her mother and, ultimately, she was led to begin a relationship with the little sister that anger and bitterness had deprived her of knowing.

She'd found the freedom of forgiveness.

THE IT FACTOR

■ FORGIVENESS

In prayer there is a connection between what God does and what you do. You can't get forgiveness from God, for instance, without also forgiving others. If you refuse to do your part, you cut yourself off from God's part. (Matthew 6:14–15 *The Message*)

Forgiveness changes us from prisoners of our past to people who are at peace with our memories. It frees us to move forward with our lives.

- Forgiveness is a choice we make that is independent of our feelings. It requires one thing: a decision to let go of a past hurt.
- Jesus tells us to forgive those who have wronged us. This is because forgiveness of other people emulates God's forgiveness of us.
- Every person has a need for forgiveness and a need to forgive. It is tempting to hold on to feelings of anger, betrayal, pain, and bitterness as a means of protecting ourselves or punishing the one who

has offended us. However, the person who *really* suffers is the one holding on to these feelings.

- When we experience hurt from someone's actions or words, we may have negative feelings such as anger, confusion, sadness, and betrayal. If we don't deal with these feelings quickly, they may gain power over us and begin to crowd out positive feelings.

- Our wounds can make us prisoners to our pasts. If we use our energy to be angry, we are unable to use that energy to reach our potential and make the most of our future. When we forgive, we allow ourselves to heal and experience peace and happiness.

- Forgiveness is not forgetfulness. Forgiveness does not mean that we deny the person's responsibility in the situation, and it doesn't minimize the wrong that was committed. The act that hurt us may always be a part of our life, but forgiveness can lessen its grip on us.

- Just as many of us need to forgive someone else, we may need to ask for forgiveness. We can also be bound to the past by our guilt and unresolved issues.

- By choosing to ask for forgiveness with a genuine and remorseful heart, we can forgive ourselves no matter how the other person reacts. We must realize that it is impossible to control anyone other than ourselves.

- When we forgive or ask for forgiveness, we do so because it is the right thing to do.

■ QUESTION

In general, is it difficult for you to forgive? Is it harder to forgive yourself or other people?

■ BENEFITS OF FORGIVENESS

If you practice forgiveness, you will experience these benefits:

- You will feel a sense of peace with God as you let go of old pain and anger.
- You will have healthier relationships as you accept yourself and others to a greater degree.
- You will be able to focus on improving yourself and your future when you are no longer focused on the past.
- You will improve your psychological well-being. You will be at lower risk for depression, anxiety, and substance abuse.
- You will be better at managing your temper. Proverbs 19:11 (AMP) tells us, "Good sense makes a man restrain his anger, and it is his glory to overlook a transgression *or* an offense."
- You will reduce the overall stress in your life which will give you improved health benefits.

Which benefit would you most desire to have? How do you see that benefit making a difference your life?

CHARACTERISTICS OF FORGIVENESS

Here are some characteristics of people who exercise forgiveness:

They let go of grudges and bitterness. As a result, they are able to focus on the future and release the pain and power of the past. They subscribe to Scriptures like Ephesians 4:31–32 (NLT):

> *Get rid of all bitterness, rage, anger, harsh words, and slander, as well as all types of evil behavior. Instead, be kind to each other, tenderhearted, forgiving one another, just as God through Christ has forgiven you.*

- They understand that forgiveness is their choice. Their decision to forgive is not based on their emotions or dependent on how they feel about someone. It is based on knowing it is the right thing to do.

- They do not expect themselves or others to be perfect. Releasing this expectation of perfection allows them to both accept and extend grace.

- They take responsibility for their own actions and ask for forgiveness from God and others if they suspect they may have hurt someone. Even if they were not the only one in the wrong or the offense was unintentional, they do not hesitate to sincerely ask for forgiveness once they are aware of the situation.

- They make an effort to understand and accept themselves and other people. They are willing to extend mercy and grace to others and themselves because God has extended it to them.

- They ask God for help when they struggle to forgive.

Do you know someone who demonstrates forgiveness? What do you admire about that person? What must you do to be more like him or her?

FORGIVENESS STEPS TO FOLLOW

Read the steps below and use them to develop a specific measurable action step to take this week.

1. **Set aside your pride.** Most of us have probably heard the saying "Fool me once, shame on you. Fool me twice, shame on me." This

is pride reinforcing the belief that we should not let others get the best of us. Likewise, pride can keep us from asking for forgiveness. Do not allow your pride to steal the freedom of forgiveness from you.

2. **Choose to forgive others.** It may be hard to forgive the person who hurt you, but you are hurting yourself and your relationship with God by holding on. Let it go.

3. **Try to understand the situation from the other person's perspective.** We are sometimes hurt by another's actions even though their intent was good. Try to understand their perspective.

4. **Realize that you may have to forgive the same offense multiple times.** Depending on the severity of the pain, you may have to make the choice to forgive several times before you are truly at peace.

5. **Ask for forgiveness.** If you are at fault for an unresolved issue in your life, go to God and to the other person and sincerely repent. Repenting is when we ask for forgiveness and proceed to change our ways. Whether or not the other person forgives you, God forgives you.

6. **Choose to forgive yourself.** It can be very difficult to forgive ourselves for our bad decisions or careless actions. Sometimes we even struggle to forgive ourselves for what we did not foresee. If you have asked for God's forgiveness, He has forgiven you. If you have trouble with this, go to God in prayer and look into His Word for comfort and confirmation. Some helpful Scriptures to meditate on are: Psalm 103; Matthew 11:28–30; John 4; and Ephesians 1 and 2.

7. **Seek counseling.** You may need outside help if the harm that was inflicted on you is more than you know how to handle. Don't be afraid to reach out for help.

You're familiar with the old written law, "Love your friend," and its unwritten companion, "Hate your enemy." I'm challenging that. I'm telling you to love your enemies. Let them bring out the best in you, not the worst. When someone gives you a hard time, respond with the energies of prayer, for then you are working out of your true selves, your God-created selves. This is what God does. He gives his best — the sun to warm and the rain to nourish — to everyone, regardless: the good and bad, the nice and nasty. If all you do is love the lovable, do you expect a bonus? Anybody can do that. If you simply say hello to those who greet you, do you expect a medal? Any run-of-the-mill sinner does that. In a word, what I'm saying is, *Grow up*. You're kingdom subjects. Now live like it. Live out your God-created identity. Live generously and graciously toward others, the way God lives toward you. (Matthew 5:43–48 *The Message*)

Share your specific action step. Remember to keep it specific by attaching a who, what, where, or when to the statement.

CHAPTER 3

THE VALUE OF RESPONSIBILITY

I love responsible people! They make life so much easier most of the time. When you look at all that the Proverbs 31 woman was involved in, her family and business activities, which included supervising servants in her home, it's obvious that she was a responsible person: a delegating, productive, and spiritually sensitive woman of God. The old adage about "if you want something done, ask a busy person" clearly applied to her. In today's terms, she would be at the top of everyone's list for chairing a fundraiser or becoming president of the parent-teacher association because she knew how to get things done.

When you think of responsibility, what comes to mind? I immediately think of those who have embraced the deep reality that their choices and behavior impacts not only them, but all who are touched by their lives.

Most of us have heard the phrase *six degrees of separation* (which describes the theory that one person knows someone who knows someone else until, through six connections, you would reach the person you were trying to reach). This theory illustrates that the world is really so much smaller than any of us realize. In the sea of billions of souls, it's amazing how our actions, through the path of six relational degrees can impact lives around the world. No, it's not just the world leaders that impact our workplace, our homes, our churches, and our schools. It really is each and every one of us.

If we truly lived from that vantage point, how different would our daily decisions be? How intent would we be in removing corruption from our own thought life? The Proverbs state quite clearly that as we think in our hearts, so we are (see Proverbs 23:7), So with that in mind, let's attempt to discern what responsibility is and what it is not.

When we think of a responsible person in the Bible, Martha, the sister of Mary and Lazarus would be a seemingly good candidate for a responsible role model. Yes? Well, yes and no.

Responsible people by nature are very astute in being problem solvers. They instinctively assume that it's better for them to be a part of the solution, rather than just a voice in the conversation. And typically, when there is a crisis, there are none better to rise to the occasion and generate a viable plan of action. However, as we examine the story of Mary and Martha in regard to their relationship with Jesus, there's a bit of a paradigm shift in perspective of how individual responsibility can look different in some areas.

We are not all the same, and our levels of responsibility within our environments need to be appreciated based on what they are. This should not be considered an excuse for a lackadaisical approach to life. We too often become so judgmental about our perception of responsibility, we leave little room for the Spirit of God to speak to us.

It is important that we realize the balance between throwing caution to the wind and being stiff as a board in this area. As we process these essential aspects of life and relationship, we must remain open to the theory of iron sharpening iron. A soft cloth can clean and shine a blade, but only friction by a like or harder material will make it a more effectual tool in the hand of a master craftsman.

As we grow and mature—physically, emotionally, and spiritually—we also grow more accountable in each of these areas. When an athlete rises to higher levels of ability through increased training and instruction, the responsibility to perform at a higher physical level is expected—and rewarded. That's why professional football players make millions, and peewee football players get an ice cream cone.

A TAKE-CHARGE WOMAN

Today in some places personal responsibility is almost looked upon with contempt. This is not a biblical principle. However, as demonstrated in the story about Jesus' relationship with Mary and Martha, we also note that the appropriate balance of *being* and *doing* requires discernment and, yes, a sense of responsibility for *greater things*.

Let's read the story of Mary and Martha in Luke 10:38–42:

> *As Jesus and his disciples were on their way, he came to a village where a woman named Martha opened her home to him. She had a sister called Mary, who sat at the Lord's feet listening to what he said. But Martha was distracted by all the preparations that had to be made. She came to him and asked, "Lord, don't you care that my sister has left me to do the work by myself? Tell her to help me!"*
>
> *"Martha, Martha," the Lord answered, "you are worried and upset about many things, but few things are needed—or indeed only one. Mary has chosen what is better, and it will not be taken away from her."*

I'm sure that we can become a bit condescending based on our personality bent. Some will say, "Martha needs to chill out. Jesus is in the house and what better investment in time than sitting at His feet and having Him speak directly into our lives?" Even He said that Mary had chosen "what is better." However, after that time of intimate learning had passed, would "what is better" possibly have shifted? Please understand, I am in no way attempting to contradict the importance of that precious affirmation from the heart of Jesus. He indeed did tell Martha that she was worried, stressed, weighed down by self-implemented expectations, but I think we can consider there is also an issue of responsibility with the time investment of the two sisters.

Timing is truly important when we look at the context of responsibility. After a big gathering, is good stewardship modeled by one person cleaning up everyone else's mess? Absolutely not. How often do we see someone use the excuse, "Well, I'm not organized, so I'm not going to worry about that." The human default is to try to bypass what we find most distasteful in respect to the duties for which we accept responsibility. And even if housework, filing, arts, music, cooking, etc. are not in our gift mix, we are responsible for implementing good delegation to the qualified. And, sometimes, we are more qualified than we realize or care to admit.

Here's an example that comes to mind. Although we didn't make the diapers that covered the bottoms of our precious children, we were responsible to make sure that a clean one was provided at the appropriate time. Our children (and their tender diaper areas), as well as society at large, were extremely grateful that we accepted responsibility to the degree we were trained and qualified. All joking aside, I believe that if Mary had continued to hang on Jesus like a rock star after He had delivered the "better" section on the evening of the dinner party, He would have graciously, in His loving way, told Mary, "Go help your sister do the dishes."

In the corporate realm, those who embrace and refine their responsibility muscles, become those who are in demand. God tells us that those who are faithful, and I dare say *responsible* is an appropriate word to insert here, with small things are given bigger assignments. The parable of the talents (Matthew 25:14–30) is a perfect example.

However, let's not leave our two sisters out of the conversation. Their responsibility quotient was in the eye of the beholder. I believe that people who needed good counsel and encouragement would have seen Mary as the responsible one — an encourager with a compassionate heart. Others would have viewed Martha as a woman of purpose and integrity, a good planner and a detailed administrator — a more stereotypical choice for the responsible one. It's not an either/or situation; it's a both/and. Both types of responsible people are essential elements in any healthy organization: family, church, work, education, and government.

There are job creators in society as well as those with the skill sets to make those business visions come to life. Is one really more important than the other? No, not in a reasonable and general context, however often those who are graced with a big vision mind-set are also the ones who take the responsibility and the big risks to provide the environment for the growth of their vision. To deny that would be like me saying, "Because I have given birth to children, that makes me a creator." I've indeed been used as a vessel of created delivery, and have accepted the responsibility for the seed that I carried. However, I didn't dream up DNA or procreation through the act of marriage. So, is my contribution as big a risk? I think not. I am responsible for my part, but for me to say that I'm equal in contribution to the visionary risk-taker, that would not only be inappropriate, but incredibly and ridiculously prideful.

Perhaps you find yourself judging others in your environment who do not embrace the same responsibilities that you do, looking at them as less important or narrow-minded? If God were to look at us in that way, we'd all be doing the same job. There would be utter chaos in that type of society. And honestly, haven't we witnessed it from elementary school sports to the global economy? It's like trying to make a chocolate cake with vanilla but no cocoa powder or melted chocolate. Yes, you'll end up with a cake, but all your good intentions will not make it what it was intended to be. To have a chocolate cake, you've got to have chocolate. If we want to achieve a specific end result, we must take responsibility to make sure all the needed ingredients are part of the mix.

Now that we've probably diverted your attention to craving something chocolate, please accept our apology and let's continue. See? We must be intentional about acting responsibly.

Responsible people also take very seriously acting on their convictions. How could we say that we are committed to education if we excuse our children from school attendance (whether public, private, or homeschooling) without appropriate reasons? How could we say we are committed to making our nation a better place if we repeatedly fail to vote in elections? How could we say we are committed to our church if we find things to do that keep us away from worship services more often than not? Responsible people put their actions where their words are.

Just a final thought about Mary and Martha. There is a time for soaking in His presence and a time to implement that soaking and invest it in others. And oddly enough, the visual of Jesus cooking on the beach in the last chapter of John reminds us that whether He was raising someone's brother from the dead or cooking a meal for beloved friends, He was always listening to His Father, and His soul was nourished by doing His will (see John 4:34).

WITHOUT EXCUSE

One of the things that I love about David's heartfelt expressions in the Psalms is his willingness to take responsibility for his failures and shortcomings. Maybe his honesty was one reason God called him "a man after my own heart" (Acts 13:22). A key to mastering and implementing the value of responsibility is to not act impulsively. But there are times when we have to "put the pedal to the metal." (Although I find that analogy unappealing, it really does define being responsible in specific situations.)

In a roundtable setting within my office, we covered this principle, and a sidebar conversation ensued after the meeting ended. A very gentle and mild woman shared that she had been given the opportunity to mentor some younger women from her religious culture. She had been born and raised in an ultraconservative Mennonite family. (In this region of the United States where we live, the Mennonite and Amish cultures happen to be closely meshed together.) She had been asked to meet with a group of young adult women who had transitioned from the Amish culture into a more evangelical Mennonite worldview. They were attempting to discern the difference between legalism and biblical doctrine, and my roundtable friend had been recommended to them.

She said that she knew immediately that this would be a wonderful opportunity to step out into an area that she had been praying about. She wanted to be on the same page as her husband, so she asked him and prayed about the opportunity. Her husband's response was to go for it, but her fear of appearing too eager held her at bay. A week went by before she contacted the woman with her yes. My friend was disappointed to find out that the young women had concluded in the meantime that they would teach themselves. She felt remorse that she hadn't embraced the opportunity in a more timely fashion. Some may say that it must not have been right for her or it would have worked out, but she feels differently. Rightly or wrongly, my friend believes that, because she didn't move on it immediately when she had confirmation in her spirit and the support of her husband, she missed her opportunity to participate in something that she'd prayed about for years.

Responsibility to evaluate and discern situations is characteristic of one who isn't afraid to stretch herself in areas of greater personal growth and influence. Our full potential cannot be reached until we are committed to taking up the mantle of responsibility that God puts before us.

Sometimes women take refuge in excuses such as "I'm not equipped" or "I've never done that before." I believe that if we are going to influence others in our workplace or at home, those excuses will wear thin very quickly — with others and with God. When God told Abraham to go to a place He would show him, *go* was the essential word.

Often it is just that simple. That's why it's so important to develop a love relationship with God. We desperately need His wisdom if we are going to understand and accept the responsibility that He reveals is His will for our life. What He directs me to do will not necessarily be anything like what He leads you to do; He has an individualized plan for each of us. Our primary task as a responsible woman is to discover His plan — and His timing — for each stage of our life and to be willing to do what He calls us to do when He tells us to do it.

When we are unwilling to take God at His Word and embrace how He is using His Holy Spirit to direct us, then we are not being responsible. Being wise, and/or sensible, is being spiritually responsible. It may seem contradictory to talk about being sensible and yet walking by faith and not by sight. However, they are not contradictory terms. God is not a God of confusion; He is a God of order, values, and principles. When He speaks and directs us to swift action, procrastination becomes nothing more than disobedience. Responsibility also takes us to a place where we won't blame circumstances or others if, for whatever reason, we fail to do what God directs.

A good friend of ours, Diane Shew, told us about something that took place years ago. It is an excellent example of someone acting on what the Holy Spirit said without understanding how God would use it.

Diane is a very intelligent woman, well-spoken and accomplished in her field. She was invited to Taiwan to speak at conference and made the trip alone. While she has a terrific sense of adventure, she found herself a little nervous and uncomfortable being in an unfamiliar place where she did not know the language. As she attempted to get through the airport and to her hotel, she searched for someone to help her find her way. Armed with her translation book, she approached a podium in the airport where a middle- aged Taiwanese woman was working. Diane began thumbing through her book looking for the words to convey what she needed.

The woman stopped her and informed Diane that she spoke English. Knowing this was unusual for a person of her age in the country at that time, Diane asked her how she came to learn the language. The woman told her that God had spoken to her about learning English and impressed on her heart that if she would invest the time to learn, He would use it for His glory. Then she smiled and said, "I learned English because God knew you would need His help today."

Diane was completely overwhelmed by this statement. At the time, she had been considering a relationship with God and had been exploring the ideas of faith and salvation through Christ. The kindness this woman showed her, coupled with her explanation that God nudged her to learn a new skill so that Diane would be taken care of, went a long way in convincing Diane that God was real and that He cared for her down to the smallest detail of helping her find her way in a foreign nation.

Today, Diane is a vibrant witness to others and helps young people develop their relationships with God. Her faith was sparked by a woman who took the responsibility to develop herself when God encouraged her to do so. Because she did, she was ready to share the love of God in a real way with Diane.

Like the Taiwanese woman, we've both learned that when God plants a desire in our hearts, even though there's no obvious timetable in sight, we need to begin preparing for a journey of faith and adventure He wants us to go on with Him.

As we have been writing this book, we have observed how before God introduced us, He was preparing us for this hour. Even before we were aware, He was molding and shaping us individually for the projects and opportunities that we would both be directly involved with, as well as those solo flights of faith where the other would stand and cheer the participant on. From business, to ministry, to music, to parenting — God has been calling us into a constant flow of opportunity predicated on our taking responsibility for what He's spoken to us in the quiet place.

One of the most important things to remember about responsibility is that God is not trying to make us miserable. His greatest desire is that we would embrace all things He sends our way in accordance with Romans 8:28 *and* 29, in order to be transformed into the image of Jesus.

THE IT FACTOR

■ RESPONSIBILITY

Make a careful exploration of who you are and the work you have been given, and then sink yourself into that. Don't be impressed with yourself. Don't compare yourself with others. Each of you must take responsibility for doing the creative best you can with your own life (Galatians 6:5 *The Message*).

We are responsible for who we become.

- Responsibility is recognizing that every decision we make affects us and the world around us and being willing to accept and own the consequences. Our decisions directly affect our outcome.

- A responsible person can be trusted and is dependable in every area of life. We can be counted on to do what we say. As responsible team members, we work hard and hold ourselves accountable for both our own results and the results of our team.

- We understand and submit to the words of Luke 12:48: "From everyone who has been given much, much will be demanded; and from the one who has been entrusted with much, much more will be asked." We know we are accountable for the abilities and resources the Lord has entrusted to us.

- When we are faced with obstacles, our first thought is to ask God for wisdom. Our second thought is to ask ourselves "what can I do" rather than dwelling on what cannot be done.

- We listen for the Spirit of God to speak to us through the Bible, in prayer, through trusted counselors, and with His "still small voice." We work to develop the things we are good at and are passionate about while trusting Him to give us opportunity to use them for His glory. When opportunity arises, we prayerfully consider and, if we accept, we do our best.

- When we are responsible, we are willing to do the right thing in spite of adversity, disappointing others, or personal sacrifice. We do not allow other people and circumstances to have control over us, our emotions, our decisions, or our future. We trust that God is in control.

- We do not make excuses or place blame on others. Instead, we look for opportunities to learn from our shortcomings and mistakes so that we can continually grow and improve.

- When we are responsible, we are faithful in serving others. We don't think: *What's in it for me?*

QUESTION:

Based on what you read above, in which ways is it easy for you to take responsibility? In what areas do you struggle?

◼ BENEFITS OF RESPONSIBLITY

When you are responsible, expect to experience these benefits:

- You will please God and He will use you in amazing ways. When you are faithful with small things, bigger opportunities will come your way. Luke 16:10–12 (NLT) says,

> *If you are faithful in little things, you will be faithful in large ones. But if you are dishonest in little things, you won't be honest with greater responsibilities. And if you are untrustworthy about worldly wealth, who will trust you with the true riches of heaven? And if you are not*

*faithful with other people's things, why should you be
trusted with things of your own?*

- You will be in demand. Others will recognize your value and will desire to have you working with them.
- You will be trusted. When you are trustworthy, you build strong relationships at home, with friends, and at work.
- You will experience personal growth and develop into your full potential in Christ. When you take ownership in your choices and learn from your mistakes, you grow as a person and become who God made you to be.
- You will develop a good reputation. As a result, your circle of influence will grow.

Which benefit would you most desire to have? How do you see that benefit making a difference in your life?

■ CHARACTERISTICS OF RESPONSIBILITY

People who practice responsibility can be recognized by these traits:
- They are big-picture thinkers. They consider long-term effects and make decisions based on their understanding of the situation in its entirety.
- They look for what they can do instead of focusing on what they have no control over.
- They are committed to finding solutions. They go beyond what is required of them and look for ways to add value and improve any situation.
- They are trustworthy. They keep their promises and fulfill their obligations.

- They are accountable and reliable. They see things through to completion.
- They do not make excuses or justify their actions. They believe the words of Galatians 6:5 (NLT): "For we are each responsible for our own conduct."
- They do what needs to be done to the best of their ability. They use all of the resources God has provided and always look to grow. They feel a sense of accomplishment when their work is complete.

■ QUESTION

Do you know someone who demonstrates responsibility? What do you admire about that person? What must you do to be more like him or her?

■ RESPONSIBILITY STEPS TO FOLLOW

Read the steps to follow below and use them to develop a specific measurable action step to take this week.

1. **Take responsibility for your life.** Commit to developing your character by fulfilling obligations. The apostle Paul urged us to use our resources and abilities to provide for ourselves.

   > *Yet we hear that some of you are living idle lives, refusing to work and meddling in other people's business. We command such people and urge them in the name of the Lord Jesus Christ to settle down and work to earn their own living* (2 Thessalonians 3:11–12 NLT).

2. **Be dependable and trustworthy.** Show up on time, keep your commitments, and follow through on your promises.

3. **Use what is in your hand.** Develop and use whatever it is that God has given to you for His glory. Do not despise small beginnings or underestimate what God can do with what He gave you. Little is much when God is in it.

4. **Find solutions.** When there is a problem, think big picture and take an active role to bring a solution. Remember to keep prayer a priority when looking for the answer.

5. **Be conscientious.** What you say and do makes a difference. Take every opportunity to be an example to and a positive influence on those around you. Look for opportunity to add value to others.

6. **Be sensible and disciplined.** Take care of your health, emotions, time, and money.

7. **Break any bad habits that keep you from being responsible.** Some examples are procrastination, blaming others, being defensive, failing to admit when you are wrong, and not making or adhering to a plan.

8. **Always do your best.** Give the best you have to everything in which you are involved. If you cannot or will not commit to give your best, it is best to not commit. We are all living representatives of Christ. To give less than our best is to do Him a disservice.

Whatever you do, work at it with all your heart, as working for the Lord, not for human masters, since you know that you will receive an inheritance from the Lord as a reward. It is the Lord Christ you are serving. (Colossians 3:23–24)

Share your specific action step. Remember to keep it specific by attaching a who, what, where, or when to the statement.

_____

_____

CHAPTER 4

THE VALUE OF ATTITUDE

Life was not easy in biblical days, even for people with servants to do the physically difficult work. Remember the description of the Proverbs 31 woman and all that she did, mentioned in our Introduction. She added to the family's income and holdings, bought or grew food and prepared it, decorated her home, and made sure members of her household had attractive, warm clothing for the winter. This was a woman who had a good attitude — she probably couldn't have gotten half of those things accomplished if she sat around feeling sorry for herself or brooding about things she might have wanted and didn't have.

Although Proverbs 31 gives a long list of this woman's material accomplishments, it saves the best for last: "a woman who fears the Lord is to be praised" (v. 30). Obviously she was a woman of spiritual depth who feared the Lord. And to be that woman she must have spent time in prayer. For us too, the depth of our preparation for all we face in life will be fashioned by our priority of communing with God. Prayer, which is pursuing a love relationship with Him by spending time discovering the secrets of His covenant (see Psalm 25:14) is essential. As essential as it is for a married woman to set aside her busy schedule and take time to speak directly and listen attentively to her husband.

The wisdom of another section of Proverbs (17:22 NLT) tells us that a cheerful heart is as good as medicine. The good medicine of employing a positive attitude is also a principle of leadership by example. However, having a cheerful heart or a good attitude may be one of the most difficult principles to practice in everyday life.

Does any of this sound familiar? You spill a quart of orange juice on the floor while making the kids' breakfast. One of your children can't find his homework. You forget where you put your cars keys, and you're already running late. It's hard not to let these frustrations jade your philosophy as the day progresses. Whether you call it "getting up on the wrong side of the bed" or "having a bad hair day," molehills can quickly become mountains.

Perhaps you had made a strategic savings plan to make a desired personal purchase, only to discover that the car is unexpectedly in need of repair. Or your child's teacher has added a resource to the reading list at the last minute. It's not only difficult to locate but extremely expensive, and there are no used editions available.

Whatever the reason we find ourselves becoming frustrated, we must remember that our attitudes influence our performance in every area of life. We have to decide, despite circumstances, are we going to give it our all or "fake it to make it"? Even when we start out with a negative outlook, we know that God has given us the capacity to turn around and walk by faith and not by sight. Ultimately, the Spirit within us can help us to persevere, and eventually prosper, in some of the most tumultuous circumstances.

In one of the Bible's most cited passages, known as the Beatitudes, we find in Jesus' words a sense of comfort, encouragement, and acceptance of even extremely difficult circumstances. Jesus said:

> *Blessed are the poor in spirit, for theirs is the kingdom of heaven. Blessed are those who mourn, for they will be comforted. Blessed are the meek, for they will*

inherit the earth. Blessed are those who hunger and thirst for righteousness, for they will be filled. Blessed are the merciful, for they will be shown mercy. Blessed are the pure in heart, for they will see God. Blessed are the peacemakers, for they will be called children of God. Blessed are those who are persecuted because of righteousness, for theirs is the kingdom of heaven. Blessed are you when people insult you, persecute you and falsely say all kinds of evil against you because of me. Rejoice and be glad, because great is your reward in heaven, for in the same way they persecuted the prophets who were before you (Matthew 5:3–12).

In that passage, we see that the true meaning of the word "blessed" has nothing to do with easy or necessarily happy circumstances for the one being blessed. In fact, the circumstances underlying the blessings which the passage describes are not the things we hope to have in our lives. But when they come — and some of them will come — what will our attitude be?

Hot water theology, as we call it, demonstrates the flavor of our attitude. Think of yourself as coffee or tea. When the steaming hot water of life pours over the depths of your being, what is the result? Something that gives others a unique taste of richness and comfort, or a bitter taste of anger and negativity.

GLORY-STRENGTH

As I write this, I am only a day removed from one of the most bittersweet events of my life. One of the people most precious to me, Faith Jones, was remembered yesterday at a celebration of an incredible life of love, service, faithfulness, and, yes, Spirit-fortified attitude. This was after a tenacious eight-year battle with breast cancer, which we had believed four years ago to be in complete remission. It reoccurred with a fierce and ravaging vengeance. There were so many times we thought, *this will probably be the last battle*, but we were wrong — until the wee hours of the morning of December 11, 2012.

Faith's overwhelming desire to choose life was one that was founded in prayer, trust in God's faithfulness, and an attitude that, although covered in a soft and gentle spirit, was one of a warrior. Funny, feminine, and favored by God with a deep wisdom, Faith not only fought her own physical battle with a dreaded malignancy but also supported her beautiful daughter, Heather, who too was battling a rare form of cancer. Heather's battle ended in December 2007 after 22 months.

Both mother and daughter had been diagnosed with their respective enemies within days of one another. However, cancer was not to be their only common legacy. Instead it was the unfathomable faith and fortitude that delivered both of them into heaven, gathering many friends along the way. *Attitude, attitude, attitude.* I was blessed to witness the outpouring of testimony at both funerals. There is no argument that each had an attitude of leadership responsibility; they were honest about the battle, but glorified God within the challenge. They left behind evidence of lives well lived.

Five years and nine days after Jesus ushered Heather into His eternal presence, He called for her mom. Faith's ministry was encouragement, and she faithfully practiced it until her dying day. Witnessing her attitude of service to her God, her family, and the extended group of friends and clients, whom she counseled professionally as long as her physical state would allow, I and others saw a shining example of a godly attitude at its best.

I was privileged to share in the counseling side of her ministry, first as a client, and then many years later (when ethically appropriate), as a ministry partner and friend. She was 17 years my senior, but she had the youthful mind-set of a peer. The benefit of life experience and education in emotional health sciences caused her to be a blessing to all who had the privilege of working with her. Her gentle and, when needed, parental-type love and wisdom, helped to form a true attitude that echoed the Beatitudes. We saw in her that blessed are those who mourn, thirst for righteousness, are poor in spirit, meek, merciful, pure in heart, and endure when suffering for their faith in God.

I had envisioned that when New Hope offered Dawn Yoder and me the opportunity to share our perspectives on "real women in the real world, making God real to others," that this chapter would be one that I could write with Faith by my side. However, because of the legacy of integrity, compassion, and wisdom that she's left with me, I will honor what God has done through her life posthumously. By reading something Faith wrote, I hope you'll get a taste of the *hot water theology* of my dear friend:

> *We pray that you'll have the strength to stick it out over the long haul — not the grim strength of gritting your teeth but the glory-strength God gives. It is strength that endures the unendurable and spills over into joy, thanking the Father who makes us strong enough to take part in everything bright and beautiful that he has for us* (Colossians 1:11–12 *The Message*).

"Glory-strength" — Now you might think that a strange phrase, but for me, I have found it to be the most descriptive phrase I have discovered to express the strength that is not our own.

It is a strength that is there in the very darkest days of our lives and souls. It is a strength that is indescribable — a strength that is incredibly beyond us.

Glory-strength is a strength that is only recognized in great sorrow or loss, in trials that seem unbearable . . . in seemingly dead-end alleys and dark dungeons (Colossians 1:13) where Paul found himself in the aloneness of tears, when nights get mixed up into days, sitting by the bedside of a loved one stricken by illness. It is there when we face the giants in our lives — death, divorce, abuse, a loved one in the bondage of addiction, financial loss, or chronic or terminal illness.

It is glory-strength "that endures the unendurable and spills over into joy." The glory-strength that moves us forward (as Peterson put it) "to take part in everything bright and beautiful that God has for us." Glory-strength does endure the unendurable, bears the unbearable and gives peace and joy in the midst of troubled waters, frantic emotions, and pleas for mercy. This was what I experienced when my daughter Heather was hundreds of miles away in the hospital facing surgery due to a rare form of cancer, and I was at home dealing with the agony of a mother's heart in not being able to be with my critically ill daughter due to my own illness. Seemingly, it was an unbearable, unendurable situation. Definitely, in the eyes of the world, but glory-strength gives vision beyond our circumstances, gives faith in the midst of the darkness and courage to go on despite our loses, and yes, even to sing and praise despite the pain and woundedness, looking forward to a day of complete healing.

What is it in your life that requires strength beyond yourself? What is it that has you so low you feel you cannot bear it? It is glory-strength that enables us to put the pieces of our lives back together. God gives to all freely. Glory-strength is there for you as it continues to be for me.

Father God, in our darkest hours You are there. Thank You for helping us to rise up when we are completely bowed down, for carrying us when we have no strength of our own, for giving us Your glory-strength. Amen.

— *Faith Jones, 2008*

Faith Jones chose to embrace a "glory-strength" attitude to see her through those dark hours. She continued to choose a thankful, God-dependent attitude after Heather's death, until the end of her own battle with breast cancer.

In reading Faith's perspective, as well as examining others throughout history, we know that attitude isn't just positive thinking. Instead, it's literally taking charge of your mind and taking hold of what God, and only God, can provide.

Paul, who suffered many setbacks and challenges as well as much resistance after his conversion, told us that we are to "take captive every thought to make it obedient to Christ" (2 Corinthians 10:5). Taking our thoughts captive means not allowing our own ambition and conceit to rule us and/or run over others. It is the attitude of those who desire God to be the center of their lives. Please be assured, as you adopt this attitude you will have opportunity to share, perhaps in a roundtable at work or in the community, how glory-strength attitudes make all the difference. Your life then will be a more of a witness to those in the unbelieving world than leaving tracts on their desks or in the restroom.

When I have faced the deaths of several loved ones, my friend Faith included, I know that the world watches as Christ followers process grief. Is our attitude a false, self-protective "it's all good cause

Jesus is in the 'hood"? Or are we real in our loss, grief, and sometimes even confusion?

Remember that even Jesus wept when Lazarus died. His attitude showed deep love for a friend, but Jesus' purpose was to do what God the Father had assigned Him to do — that meant raising Lazarus from the dead. Knowing all things, Jesus knew He was bringing Lazarus from a better place back to a sinful world where one day he would have to die again. Maybe that knowledge brought His tears.

A WILLING WOMAN

To see a biblical example of a woman with a godly attitude, we only have to look as far as the four-chapter Book of Ruth. Although Ruth lived in Moab, she had married a Jewish man living in her country. During a relatively short period of time, her husband, her brother-in-law, and her father-in-law died. Her mother-in-law, Naomi, decided to return to her homeland of Israel. Orpah, Ruth's sister-in-law, and Ruth started to go with Naomi. But after Naomi urged them to stay in their country, Orpah turned around and went home. It was at that point that Ruth swore she would stay with Naomi with that wonderful declaration (often borrowed to use in wedding vows):

> *Don't urge me to leave you or to turn back from you.*
> *Where you go I will go, and where you stay I will stay.*
> *Your people will be my people and your God my God.*
> *Where you die I will die, and there I will be buried. May*
> *the LORD deal with me, be it ever so severely, if even*
> *death separates you and me (Ruth 1:16–17).*

Read the rest of the Book of Ruth and you'll discover that Ruth, who had been a pagan, accepted Naomi's God, Jehovah, and worshipped Him. When they arrived in Israel, Ruth followed Naomi's instructions and gleaned in the fields to gather food for them, as the destitute were allowed to do. But even that was part of God's plan. As she worked in the fields, God brought her to the attention of Boaz, a wealthy landowner who fell in love and soon married her. They had a son, Obed, who became the grandfather of King David. That meant that Ruth became one of the ancestors of Jesus Christ (Matthew 1:5–6).

There is also another attitude on display in the Book of Ruth. In their past Naomi must have lived out her faith enough to attract Ruth to it but, after her husband and both sons died, her attitude had become one of self-pity and negativity. When they moved back to Bethlehem she asked people to call her *Mara*, which means "bitter," instead of *Naomi*, which means "pleasant." Her reason: "The Lord has afflicted me; the Almighty has brought misfortune upon me" (Ruth 1:21). At that point Naomi needed an attitude adjustment. She got it as she saw Ruth's willingness to do anything necessary to help her and God's ultimate provision for both of them.

By the end of the book, we see that not only has Ruth been blessed but Naomi has been blessed because of her. As Naomi holds her new grandson, the women of the town praise the Lord for all He had done for her (4:14–15). No more talk of "call me Bitter."

INTO UNCHARTED TERRITORY

If Lewis and Clark had let the attitudes of fear of the unknown or fear of failure dominate their lives, the names of Lewis and Clark wouldn't be recorded in every American history book. Instead, they set off to chart the unknown western part of the United States — and the rest is history.

How about the apostles? How did their attitude toward the future impact their decisions? Peter knew that he would meet a demise that no one would choose. Jesus told him that he would be taken where he did not want to go (John 21:18). (And tradition says that he was crucified upside down next to his wife.) His love for Jesus and the assurance of an eternal reward helped him to go boldly forward preaching the gospel.

The Book of Acts demonstrates the power of the Holy Spirit and reiterates through the stories of many the importance of having an attitude willing to receive what God has appointed for us. We see in these accounts people who lived lives dependent on God, regardless of their circumstances. And even when faced with making a choice about their own well-being, their attitude toward God's truth took them outside themselves. They demonstrated their willingness to pioneer uncharted territory. Not because it looked easy, but because their attitude toward God required them to walk by faith and not by sight.

What about the uncharted territory of suffering? Do I believe that God deliberately inflicts disease on people such as my friend Faith? Not really. However, if we submit to Him in spite of circumstances, He is faithful to honor our desire to bless Him, bless others, and represent the truth of a kingdom-focused attitude.

Ultimately, if Jesus is the Lord of our life, we have the opportunity to exhibit a faith-focused attitude when seeing problems as opportunities to learn, looking for creative solutions to problems, and embracing the mind of Christ that is within us. When we adopt this attitude, He allows us to have a perfect peace, even in the midst of life's storms, as we place our trust in His character and faithfulness (Isaiah 26:3–4).

THE IT FACTOR

■ ATTITUDE

Always be humble and gentle. Be patient with each other, making allowance for each other's faults because of your love. Make every effort to keep yourselves united in the Spirit, binding yourselves together with peace. For there is one body and one Spirit, just as you have been called to one glorious hope for the future. There is one Lord, one faith, one baptism, and one God and Father, who is over all and in all and living through all. . . . Since you have heard about Jesus and have learned the truth that comes from him, throw off your old sinful nature and your former way of life, which is corrupted by lust and deception. Instead, let the Spirit renew your thoughts and attitudes. (Ephesians 4:2–6, 21–23 NLT)

A good attitude changes your life.

- Our attitude should reflect the attitude that is demonstrated by Jesus. Over and over in the Scriptures, we see His heart for people — how He loved them, saw and encouraged their potential, offered them a second chance, and served them with humility. We also witness how He lived with courage, faith, and commitment to do the Father's will even though it meant making payment for the sins of the world.
- Attitude is a daily choice. The attitude we choose determines how we will learn, serve, listen, and make changes throughout our lives.
- "Attitude is a little thing, which makes a big difference" (Winston Churchill). It is the foundation for success.
- The right attitude involves taking charge of our minds. Being positive is more than just repeating words of affirmation. It is having the courage, persistence, and discipline to change what we do not like or to change the way we think about it if it is something over which we do not have control.

- When we look for the opportunity in every situation, we give ourselves a chance to grow and learn from the people or circumstances involved. What we learn may have a lifelong impact.
- Maturity and success come when we submit our mind to God and overcome attitudes of self-pity, selfishness, and other negative ways of thinking.

■ QUESTION

Were you raised in an environment where a positive attitude was encouraged?

■ BENEFITS OF A POSITIVE ATTITUDE

You will reap many benefits from having a positive attitude:

- You will be happy and energized.
- You will trust in God and not carry the weight of the world on your shoulders. You will leave the heavy lifting to Him.
- You will focus on the present and find growth opportunities in problems.
- You will learn from your failures rather than being defeated by them. Every time you make a mistake or are not perfect at something, you will be able to learn from it and then allow God to take you to the next place rather than being afraid to try again.
- You will reach your goals more quickly and easily.
- Others will start to reflect your attitude. Your attitude is contagious!

Which benefit would you most desire to have? How do you see that benefit making a difference your life?

■ CHARACTERISTICS OF A POSITIVE ATTITUDE

People who practice a good attitude can be recognized by these traits:

- They approach tasks with a good outlook and choose to look for the best in people and situations. Every experience is worthwhile because it gives them an opportunity to grow and share who Christ is with others.

> *Do everything readily and cheerfully — no bickering, no second-guessing allowed! Go out into the world uncorrupted, a breath of fresh air in this squalid and polluted society. Provide people with a glimpse of good living and of the living God. Carry the light-giving Message into the night so I'll have good cause to be proud of you on the day that Christ returns. You'll be living proof that I didn't go to all this work for nothing* (Philippians 2:14–16 *The Message*).

- They minimize fear before they face problems because problems have a purpose and bring opportunity.
- They learn from their mistakes and then let them go.
- They look for creative solutions when difficult circumstances arise. They constantly think about what they can do rather than what they cannot do.
- They worship, praise, and trust God. They believe He has great plans for them and live accordingly.
- They do not give up easily; they make it a point to stay focused and optimistic.
- They frequently evaluate and adjust their attitude. They know that worry, pressure, illness, and difficulties can affect their disposition. They give these things over to God and rely on Him to align their minds with His truth.

■ QUESTION

Do you know someone who has a great attitude? What do you admire about that person? What must you do to be more like him or her?

■ ATTITUDE STEPS TO FOLLOW

Read the steps to follow below and use them to develop a specific measurable action step to take this week.

1. **Choose to maintain a positive attitude.** Discipline yourself to look for the good in situations and in others.

2. **Praise God regardless of your circumstances.** No matter how difficult life becomes, He is worthy to be praised just because He is the Lord. A thankful heart helps us to keep a right attitude.

> *I bless GOD every chance I get; my lungs expand with his praise. I live and breathe GOD; if things aren't going well, hear this and be happy: Join me in spreading the news; together let's get the word out. GOD met me more than halfway, he freed me from my anxious fears. Look at him; give him your warmest smile. Never hide your feelings from him. When I was desperate, I called out and GOD got me out of a tight spot. GOD's angel sets up a circle of protection around us while we pray. Open your mouth and taste, open your eyes and see—how good GOD is. Blessed are you who run to him. Worship GOD if you want the best; worship opens doors to all his goodness* (Psalm 34:1–9 The Message).

3. **Do what you know to be right.** Doing what is right makes you feel good and produces good outcomes. It is much easier to stay positive when you have something to be positive about.

4. **Have a clear vision of the purpose for your life.** Follow the leadings of God and search for the specifics that will get you closer to reaching your goals. Then align your behavior to match.

5. **Give yourself an attitude check when you are under pressure.** Learn to discern negative signs. Some signs of negativism are: pessimism, impatience, lack of motivation, and apathy. If you discover these things in yourself, ask God for forgiveness and take the initiative to adjust your attitude.

6. **Take in positive material.** Discipline yourself not to spend time watching, reading, or listening to things that put you in a negative or non-Christlike frame of mind.

7. **Surround yourself with people who have a positive attitude.** It is very difficult to remain positive if you are constantly immersed in negativity.

8. **Submit your attitudes to the Word of God.** Meditate on the Scripture to become like-minded with Christ. Allow the words of truth to shape who you are, how you view the world around you, and your behavior.

> *Summing it all up, friends, I'd say you'll do best by filling your minds and meditating on things true, noble, reputable, authentic, compelling, gracious — the best, not the worst; the beautiful, not the ugly; things to praise, not things to curse. Put into practice what you learned from me, what you heard and saw and realized. Do that, and God, who makes everything work together, will work you into his most excellent harmonies* (Philippians 4:8–9 *The Message*).

Share your specific action step. Remember to keep it specific by attaching a who, what, where or when to the statement.

CHAPTER 5

THE VALUE OF RESOLVING CONFLICT

As we observe the life of the Proverbs 31 woman, nothing is said about conflict. She seems to have almost an idealistic, peaceful life, but let's be realistic. She had servants. Female servants. So the reality of her life would have involved occasionally breaking up arguments or fights or at least trying to reconcile co-workers whose disagreements had escalated. And she had children. What mother hasn't had to intercede to break up sibling rivalry-inspired fights or arguments?

I smile as I write this because the images of interactions around high school locker rooms (yes, there are "mean girls"), women's ministry events, and after-Christmas sales also come flooding into my thoughts. While *real women* don't engage in physical catfights (such as those portrayed in B movies), there are situations where we have a responsibility to step in, even if it involves conflict.

As much as we would like to, none of us can avoid conflict, but we can take a fresh look at how this does not have to be a negative issue. Learning to resolve conflict in a healthy way can help us grow both personally and in relationship with others. It can also assist us in accomplishing greater things.

Wherever there is more than one person, there is the potential for conflict. Often the origin of the outward conflict stems from the conflict that dwells within the wells of the human heart. We want to be valued, appreciated, respected, and loved. And we want to be right! The conflict within our own souls, mingled with pride, can birth a perfectly volatile playground for destructive conflict.

Jesus told us that there would always be wars and conflicts while we reside on earth. However, His assurance that He has overcome the world (John 16:33), and that through Him we, too, can become overcomers, should help us embrace a healthier attitude toward those conflicts that are inevitable.

Is conflict always negative? It really doesn't have to be a destructive tool in the enemy's hands. Again, the reminder that our need for validation and *winning* in the selfish sense, can be a detriment. We have to make a choice to engage in conflict. And most assuredly, there is a time for it. For without it we become less of who we ultimately are destined to become.

Sometimes the events surrounding a conflict are our responsibility. We choose unwisely and then attempt to defend the ill-advised decision with bravado and justification. Nothing within those ugly, emotional parameters depicts anything birthed by the Spirit of God within us.

In the marketplace we will, sometimes on a daily basis, be faced with leading, equipping, correcting, and forgiving those who hold none of our beliefs as their own. Of course, this could be a stage for all-out war, unless we learn how to manage conflict effectively.

WARRING WOMEN

As anyone who has been a church member for long knows, the body of Christ is a kaleidoscope of colors and facets. It contains personalities of all types, people from all sorts of backgrounds who may have difficulty seeing life through the eyes of another. That is why, even a Christian with the best of intentions, can have conflict with another Christian with equally good intentions. In areas where the Bible doesn't give exact guidance, the possibility of a conflict is always there. The early church had its share of warring factions within its congregations. Paul addressed one particular conflict directly by calling out two women by name when he wrote to the Philippian church:

> *I plead with Euodia and I plead with Syntyche to be of the same mind in the Lord. Yes, and I ask you, my true companion, help these women since they have contended at my side in the cause of the gospel* (Philippians 4:2–3).

Note that Paul doesn't take sides in whatever the disagreement was, although he had undoubtedly been told about it. He recognizes that both of these women have been helpful to him in spreading the gospel. Maybe the conflict wasn't one that had an easily discernible right or wrong to it. While Paul doesn't take sides, he asks them to let the Lord take over and for them to get on the same side: "to be of the same mind in the Lord." That may have involved, as it sometimes does, one person giving up the right to be right and allowing the other person to have a seeming *win*. However, what Paul seems to be asking is that both women immediately agree to drop their hostility, which was undoubtedly causing problems in the church. Paul asked his friend, "my true companion," to step in as a mediator to help resolve the conflict.

We can only hope Paul's wise advice was followed about 2,000 years ago, saving a mar on the reputation of an otherwise good church. Regardless of whether those women resolved their conflict on earth, they found when they reached heaven that there is no such thing as a conflict there.

CONFLICT IN TODAY'S WORLD

Believing the truth of what Scripture teaches is essential to embracing how God wants us to be used to bless, and to be blessed, during times of conflict. If we subscribe to Paul's assertion that in our weakness, God exhibits His strength (2 Corinthians 12:9), then we are well on our way to successfully keeping conflict in proper perspective.

We can choose to allow the gentle, yet firm, touch of the heavenly Potter's hand to direct and mold us into the optimal vessel for greater use. Taking the analogy of pottery further, conflict unaddressed is like drinking from a mug with a jagged imperfection on the rim. Eventually, it's going to cut the one who uses it. How disappointing to choose an attractive mug, fill it with coffee, raise the mug to your lips — and draw blood. Obviously, if the potter shaping a mug notes an imperfection in the clay and can make the needed repair before the vessel is fired, everyone wins. The vessel is valued rather than discarded, the recipient is refreshed, and the potter is credited with creating a delivery system for the needs of the day.

Just as there is a time when a problem can be avoided in pottery making, in every environment a breakdown in communication that was not repaired early appears to be the most insidious root of conflict. If you have an argument with your husband about an issue that seems to arise time after time, it's an indication of unresolved conflict. If a co-worker keeps making the same mistake but does nothing to change the habit that negatively impacts an individual or department — and there is no supervisory intervention — again there's unresolved conflict.

Some personalities seem to thrive on negative conflict because they have not come from an environment where open and honest communication was part of the landscape. Individuals from these families or workplaces have found a way, although a negative one, to express their own unaddressed emotional disappointments. Countless physical and emotional health issues, and dare I say spiritual as well, could find rapid resolution except for the presence of perpetual negative conflict in the life of that individual.

Having emotionally mature measures of identifying conflict and addressing it appropriately brings freedom to those in the midst of the storm. So often, for instance, when people pursue counseling, it's an outlet for them to voice and process the conflict in their given situation. Professional, pastoral, and lay counselors have all empowered timid individuals to address core issues of conflict. During counseling they are able to state the facts of a conflict, which enables the counselor to help them identify where communication, or lack thereof, came off the rails. Those who have a humble attitude will be far more successful in finding solutions that everyone can live with. It doesn't mean everyone is going to be happy with the result, but even in the midst of disappointing outcomes, relationships can remain intact. And in the long term, that truly is a win/win.

What we see so often when there is a conflict is that inappropriate behavior is accepted or tolerated in the hope of avoiding offense. Meanwhile, as we keep stuffing emotions, we are inching down the road of division instead of unity.

In trying to resolve conflict, we can share our thoughts, ideas, beliefs, and convictions without being manipulative or aggressive. Assertiveness is not negative. It's a character trait that allows others to be confident that they know who they are dealing with. It's honesty. I've learned that in the business world one of greatest challenges is to speak truthfully and maintain integrity when I feel that I am the odd woman out on theological, political, or moral issues. However, if I don't speak up with integrity, I can only imagine the countless opportunities I will miss later on when someone looking for an honest opinion will not think of me as the one to approach.

THE IT FACTOR

■ RESOLVING CONFLICT

Strive for peace with everyone, and for the holiness without which no one will see the Lord. See to it that no one fails to obtain the grace of God; that no "root of bitterness" springs up and causes trouble, and by it many become defiled. (Hebrews 12:14–15 ESV)

Conflict will occur, but a war does not have to ensue.

- Life will never be completely without conflict.
- Often conflict arises as our ideas clash with other people's ideas and opinions. A major part of our lives is spent learning how to present our ideas and how to react to the ideas and opinions of others.
- Internal conflict is another area we must deal with. Often the things we want, want to say, or want to do conflict with what we know we should want, say, and do. When this happens, it can set us on edge and make us difficult to deal with. James 4:1 (ESV) asks: *"What causes quarrels and what causes fights among you? Is it not this, that your passions are at war within you?"* The only way to solve this conflict is to submit ourselves to God and immerse ourselves in His ways. The only way to become like Jesus is to spend more time with Him.
- Sometimes conflict occurs because of the condition of our world. Each of us is influenced by either the powers of darkness or the Spirit of God. It is important to keep this in mind when conflict occurs as it can help us to view a situation or person through God's eyes.

For we are not fighting against flesh-and-blood enemies,
but against evil rulers and authorities of the unseen

world, against mighty powers in this dark world, and against evil spirits in the heavenly places (Ephesians 6:12 NLT).

- We can learn from experiences of conflict and gain great wisdom. Conflict can be a catalyst for us to be able to grow or make progress. Through this process, we discover our strengths and weaknesses.
- Some people think that by addressing a conflict, they are creating one, so they keep quiet when upset. This does not resolve conflict, it just hides it for a while. Unresolved conflict can lead to resentment and drive a permanent wedge into a relationship.
- We can choose to let conflict polish our character, or we can allow it to make us angry at life. We can be humble and thankful and learn from it or be critical, haughty, and arrogant. The attitude you choose will directly affect your outcome.

■ QUESTION

Do you embrace conflict, brace yourself for conflict, or avoid conflict?

■ BENEFITS OF RESOLVING CONFLICT

There are several benefits to be gained by being able to resolve conflict well:

- You will experience God's blessing. Jesus taught us in Matthew 5:9 (*The Message*): "You're blessed when you can show people how to cooperate instead of compete or fight. That's when you discover who you really are, and your place in God's family." Resolving conflict creates a way for peace.
- You will learn other people's perspectives on problems and situations.

- Dealing with conflict requires creativity, reason, and discernment in order to overcome and resolve the issue.
- You will build stronger relationships by keeping open communication and being respectful of the other person's opinion.
- You will grow and progress as a person and become a problem solver rather than someone who is contributing to the problem.
- You will alleviate the stress and tension associated with having unresolved conflict.

Which benefit would you most desire to have? How do you see that benefit making a difference your life?

■ CHARACTERISTICS OF RESOLVING CONFLICT

When people resolve conflict well:

- Their motive is love. They want to resolve conflict in order to restore relationship and harmony.
- They are good listeners. They allow other people to feel heard and valued.
- They approach the problem from a place of humility and desire to hear and understand the other side of the story or another person's viewpoint.
- They keep a good attitude and refrain from sarcastic remarks or verbal attacks during discussions. They ask God to help them with both their understanding and their words.

> *"Let your speech always be gracious, seasoned with salt, so that you may know how you ought to answer each person"* (Colossians 4:6 ESV).

- They express opinions in an open and calm manner. They give reasons and logic for their point of view.
- They do not fear altering their opinions once they have listened to the other party's perspective and reasoning. They truly desire what is best overall for everyone involved.

■ QUESTION:

Do you know someone who resolves conflict well? What do you admire about that person? What must you do to be more like him or her?

■ RESOLVING CONFLICT STEPS TO FOLLOW

Read the steps to follow below and use them to develop a specific measurable action step to take this week.

1. **Be committed to humility.** Regardless of if you are right or wrong, humility is a becoming trait. It keeps you from alienating yourself from others and ensures you approach others with the right attitude. *"All of you, clothe yourselves with humility toward one another, because, 'God opposes the proud but shows favor to the humble.' Humble yourselves, therefore, under God's mighty hand, that he may lift you up in due time"* (1 Peter 5:5–6).

2. **Remember that being right is not more important than damaging a relationship.** Do not sacrifice a relationship just to have the satisfaction of hearing that you were right. Resolving conflict is not about getting the *win*. It is about bringing peace.

3. **Attempt to resolve the conflict in a timely manner.** We are going to get angry sometimes, but it is important to not let it take hold of our hearts and minds. Ephesians 4:26 (*The Message*) urges us to *"Go ahead and be angry. You do well to be angry — but don't use your anger as fuel for revenge. And don't stay angry. Don't go to bed angry. Don't give the Devil that kind of foothold in your life."*

4. **Know how you feel and why you feel that way before you engage in conflict.** Knee-jerk reactions or speaking before you think will only increase the tension in a conflict. It may be helpful to write down some key points before you address the other person.

5. **Be a good listener.** It is vital to understand the other person's perspective. Helping the other person to feel heard and understood can go a long way in resolving the conflict. Do not listen in order to answer, listen in order to understand.

6. **Keep an open mind during communication.** Do not become defensive or shut down. Sometimes everything within in you just wants the conflict to stop, so you stop listening and participating. There are situations where that may be the wisest thing to do temporarily. But if the relationship is important to you, you cannot leave it hanging forever without creating permanent damage.

7. **Exercise restraint.** If a conflict is becoming heated, take a breath, say a prayer, act in a way that Jesus would. You can choose to refuse to allow a battle to escalate into a war.

8. **Say what is on your mind.** Speak in a way that is clear and assertive without being aggressive and manipulating. When you manipulate others, you may get your way, but the conflict is not resolved.

> *Post this at all the intersections, dear friends: Lead with your ears, follow up with your tongue, and let anger straggle along in the rear. God's righteousness doesn't grow from human anger. So throw all spoiled virtue and cancerous evil in the garbage. In simple humility, let our gardener, God, landscape you with the Word, making a salvation-garden of your life*
>
> (James 1:19–21 *The Message*).

Share your specific action step. Remember to keep it specific by attaching a who, what, where or when to the statement.

_____

_____

_____

_____

_____

_____

_____

_____

_____

_____

_____

_____

_____

_____

_____

_____

_____

_____

_____

_____

Chapter 6

The Value of Restraint

The Proverbs 31 woman must have been one who could both restrain her tongue and her actions. How do we know? The first things that are said about her are she is a woman of "noble character" (v. 10) and "her husband has full confidence in her and lacks nothing of value. She brings him good, not harm, all the days of her life" (vv. 11–12). A little later the author tells us that this woman's "husband is respected at the city gate where he takes his seat among the elders of the land" (v. 23). If she had been a gossip or a busybody, she would not have been said to have a "noble character." If she had been morally loose in any way, she would have done him harm and not good. By the effect her words and actions had on her husband — who held an office like today's politicians — we know a lot about her. Lack of restraint was not a problem for her.

I wish I could say the same for myself. I cannot remember how many times I wished that I had waited an additional five seconds before sharing a response in a conversation, reaction in an argument, comment when teaching, or request in prayer. In just five seconds of silence, tremendously different results can occur. In just five seconds of seeking the Lord's will over my own, what He desires can be better accomplished. Too often I find that I first say what I think is right and then ask Him to bless what I have chosen in my own wisdom and strength. Time and time again, it has been obvious that this is not the best way.

Proverbs 21:2 (ESV) tells us, "Every way of a man is right in his own eyes, but the Lord weighs the hearts." In this verse lies such a valuable reminder. We all *think* the first thing that enters our mind in any given situation is right. After all, we are more likely to believe ourselves than we are to believe anyone else. What we sometimes fail to take into consideration is the strong influence of our unique emotions, inclinations, experiences, and sinful nature. All we process comes through our own individualized filter. Sometimes our filter is dirty, torn, or in need of replacement, greatly hindering our ability to process a situation from a healthy or unbiased point of view. Before we even realize it, an off-the-cuff response comes forth, potentially impacting a situation to an undesirable degree.

It is vitally important that we take those extra five seconds, and oftentimes longer, to submit ourselves to the Lord before we respond. By doing this we allow Him to weigh our hearts with His scales of knowledge, wisdom, and truth. When we use restraint in our words instead of just speaking our first thought, we are submitting both our thoughts and words to a divine filter. We are giving the Lord permission to influence and shape what will come forth. This kind of purposeful submission invites the Lord to be a part of everything we say. When He speaks through us, instead of us speaking for ourselves, things tend to go much more smoothly than they would otherwise.

This is also an issue for me when I pray. "Even in prayer you use restraint?" you might ask in shock. Yes, even here. I know that God knows everything that is on my mind before I verbally present it to Him. But I believe that in the place of prayer, I should show restraint in what and how I pray over situations, myself, and others. It seems wise to me not just to blurt out my feelings. Instead I ask the Lord to lead and guide me as I share my heart with Him.

There is no doubt that He can handle my little snits, outbursts, and self-indulgent whining sessions. In fact, He has been quite longsuffering when it has come to these episodes over the years. Thankfully, He knows that I'm "but dust" and keeps that frailty in perspective as He restrains His discipline in dealing with me for my own self-focused tendencies. A reminder to me that He is a kind, gracious, and merciful Father.

I don't think it is a surprise to the Lord that we struggle in this area. It is fairly obvious it has always been this way. James 1:19–20 states, "My dear brothers and sisters, take note of this: Everyone should be quick to listen, slow to speak and slow to become angry, because human anger does not produce the righteousness that God desires." It is important to remember that when we allow our own words to take precedence, we have placed the Lord's words and wisdom on the back burner.

I'm not God — thank goodness for that! And admittedly, often I act nothing like Him. But I'm learning. Understanding and applying the principle of restraint is a life-transforming process that, when practiced regularly, can produce some incredible results.

A JUDICIOUS WOMAN

Abigail is a stellar example of a woman who knew how to control herself, including her tongue. We find her in 1 Samuel 25 living with her husband, Nabal, whose name aptly means "fool." Scripture tells us that he was also surly and mean (v. 3). So you can imagine the kind of home life that Abigail endured.

Nabal shows his meanness when he's brought a message by his servants. David the anointed future king is on the run from King Saul who is trying to kill him. While Nabal's flocks were being sheared, David and his men had protected them from thieves and did not take anything for themselves, as often happened. The traditional response to such kindness would be for the landowner to send out food and wine to the band of men. But when David sent a message to Nabal asking for that hospitality, Nabal flatly refused and sent a harsh message back. When David gets the rebuke, he has 400 of his men sword-up and get ready to attack Nabal's estate.

Meanwhile Abigail has heard from her servants about the insult. Without her husband's knowledge, she has her servants quickly gather massive amounts of food and take them to David's men. Then she follows on her donkey.

After Abigail reaches David, she humbly pleads for forgiveness and for the lives of her household (which included her husband). She asks David to exercise restraint because otherwise he will put himself in the wrong and the Lord will not be able to bless him in the future. David is so impressed by Abigail that he says (1 Samuel 25:33–35):

> *May you be blessed for your good judgment and for keeping me from bloodshed this day and from avenging myself with my own hands. Otherwise, as surely as the* Lord, *the God of Israel, lives, who has kept me from harming you, if you had not come quickly to meet me, not one male belonging to Nabal would have been left alive by daybreak." Then David accepted from her hand what she had brought him and said, "Go home in peace. I have heard your words and granted your request."*

When Abigail returned home, she also used restraint. She might have wanted to let her foolish husband know how close he had come to destroying their household, but he was so drunk that she waited. The next morning she told him and the shock caused a heart attack or stroke (v. 38). Ten days later he died. God removed Nabal from Abigail's life and gave her a new husband — a young, handsome man who would soon be king. The one she had taught a valuable lesson on restraint.

A RESTRAINING INFLUENCE

There is absolutely no way to sustain the call to "ignite transformation" that we've talked about in this book without being appropriately restrained. A life which consistently demonstrates restraint is a life which cries out to the Father, "You can trust me." A life lived within the principle of restraint is a life which invites the favor and blessing of God.

Our words are powerful. The words that we speak to ourselves about ourselves and the words we speak to others. Proverbs 18:21 reminds us, "The tongue has the power of life and death, and those who love it will eat its fruit." Our words can be used either to build others up or tear them down. We have the ability to ignite transformation both in ourselves and others when we are willing to speak words of life over any given individual or situation.

My heart wells with thanksgiving when I reflect on all the times God has not only restrained horrific consequences in my life, but also where He has restrained blessings that would have developed a self-centered bratty result in me. I am thankful that He loves me so much that even when I do not understand, or perhaps even agree with, the way circumstances play out in my life or business, I can be assured that His heart is for me and He is always on my side.

Although many would agree that restraint practiced in our homes, churches, workplaces and communities would be helpful, what we often see is the opposite of restraint. Many in society today have thrown self-restraint under the bus. Our tremendous national debt is only one of the woes that plague us in the United States. Unwed and unwanted pregnancies abound. Teenagers bully each other through social media. Third-graders carry smartphones. Obesity is an epidemic. Everywhere we look we see the unpleasant consequences of lifestyles characterized by a lack of restraint — self-restraint or parental restraint. The consequences can be deadly and self-perpetuating. The next generations are being shaped and molded by an unspoken philosophy of, "If you've got it, flaunt it, and if you haven't got it, do whatever it takes to get it — no matter what the cost!" While some of these woes are financial and some are moral — all have the base cause of lack of restraint being practiced, modeled, or taught.

JUDICIOUS WOMEN

Those who must deal with the consequences brought about by refusing to practice restraint see the woes of society. One woman whom we respect greatly is our friend, Linda. She is a juvenile court judge who has been on the bench for several years and is one of the most levelheaded people we've ever met. Although she is very discreet in sharing the woes she witnesses and must pass judgment upon as part of her job, it's easy to recognize how they affect the heart of this dedicated public servant. Yes, she is a Christ follower working in the dark recesses of the real world. However, she has not become cynical or fatalistic because she knows that there is an opportunity for a life to be transformed when people, young and not so young, learn to make choices based on values and principles.

Over the years that we've known Linda, we've come to understand why she is such an accomplished judicial influence where she serves.

Besides principled thinking and integrity, she exudes hope — a hope that if individuals will admit that the choices that brought them into her courtroom will not serve them well if continued, they will have a good chance at a second chance. She has an "Iron Lady" dedication to justice, mixed with a compassionate heart, often seen in the countless mission activities she's supported with her treasure, talents, and time.

Undoubtedly, there are some who have vehemently disagreed with her judgments as they stood before her bench, perhaps parents who thought she was merciless while handing down a consequence for their child's actions. However, because she does in fact demonstrate restraint in her conduct and speech and does not waste her influence with idle words, she knows when to listen and when to speak. She not only has been an increasingly positive influence in the community but now is connected with other women dedicated to making a difference for the kingdom. We rejoice when we see such qualities of influence, restraint, and honesty coming from someone who has a worldview that is much different from other women in corporate or domestic environments.

Our friend Linda is one who spurs us to think before we act and speak. She serves in her courtroom with great humility and conviction. Although no parent wants to be in the situation where his or her child would have to stand before a juvenile court judge, we are confident that every person who comes before her bench is treated as if they have value. I'd trust her for a fair and just judgment if someone I loved stood before her. We are thankful to know that there are judges who are not tainted by conceit and selfish ambition, who aren't passing judgments based on a heightened view of their own power.

Linda reminds us of a woman in the Old Testament who was also a judge, Deborah (Judges 4). She led the nation of Israel in the early days after they entered the Promised Land. In those days, the judges were the rulers because there was no king. It was an incredibly bad time in which surrounding enemies continually attacked them. When Deborah told her chief general, Barak, to attack the Canaanites, he seemed to have a problem with courage. He said, "If you go with me, I will go; but if you don't go with me I won't go" (4:8). She went — and they had a great victory.

More problematic than a general's cowardice was the attitude of the people. Forgetting the blessings that God had given them as He brought them out of slavery in Egypt and into the Promised Land, the new generations didn't know the Lord. They had fallen into idolatry and sinfulness (2:10–17). The key verse of Judges says it all: "Everyone did what was right in his own eyes" (15:6; 21:25). Because Deborah ruled righteously and bravely she was able to restrain some of the evil going on in the land. Under her rule, the people enjoyed peace for 40 years.

ROYAL RESTRAINT

We saw an example from David's life in our section on Abigail, "A Judicious Woman," in this chapter. It's interesting that David could show great restraint sometimes — and show very little at other times (like most of us). In 1 Samuel 24 David was fleeing the insane, murderous jealousy of King Saul. When Saul heard that David was in the Desert of En Gedi, he took 3,000 men to hunt him down. Saul happened to go into a dark cave for a bathroom break. David and his men were hiding in that cave, and David was able to sneak up close enough to cut off a piece of Saul's robe. He showed restraint because he could have murdered Saul in the cave. Later David showed that piece of cloth to Saul to prove that he could have easily killed him but refrained. David not only demonstrated his ability to restrain himself, but also his respect for God's anointing of Saul as king. David chose to wait on God to remove Saul.

We could learn a valuable lesson from David. Though he knew that he had been anointed by the Lord to be the next king, he recognized the importance of "giving honor where honor is due" until the appointed time. Too many times within the realms of society, business, and the church body, we see a lack of restraint demonstrated. For instance, how many times has someone been placed in leadership who, over a period of time, proves not to have been the best choice for the job? Often this is handled improperly and in a way that does not honor the Lord, the person in question, or the authority of the leadership who put the person in that position. Gossip, strife, and backbiting (fruits of a lack of restraint) often rear their ugly head in these situations.

A need for understanding the principle of recognizing and honoring the position of authority, rather than the person who has been given that authority is key. When we honor the Lord by submitting to the authority that has been placed over us, whether we like it or not, we position ourselves for continued favor and blessing. In doing this we declare through our actions of restraint that although we recognize the need for change, we also trust the Lord that He will position us appropriately in His perfect timing.

Unfortunately, David after his assent to the throne of Israel did not continue in that practice of self-restraint. His lack of restraint of passion and his attempt to deceive his subjects is recorded in 2 Samuel 11. By committing adultery with Bathsheba, getting her pregnant, and then sending her husband Uriah to the front lines of battle to be killed, David became an example of how lack of self-restraint can affect our lives and the lives of those around us.

After David found out that Bathsheba was pregnant, he brought Uriah home from the battlefield for a night so that he would sleep with his wife and think the baby was his. Ironically, Uriah had such integrity and self-restraint that he refused to spend the night with his wife while his comrades remained on the battlefield. (Was King David surprised to find such depth of character in the husband whose wife he had taken?) Rather than repent of his sin, David went further to cover it up. He had Uriah carry his own sealed death order back to the front lines. It's sad to think that Uriah suffered and died because of his good character, but in that situation who would you rather be? Uriah or David? I vote for Uriah.

However, before we get too self-righteous about David's lack of self-control, let's think of our own shortcomings. In the same way that David was unable to revoke Uriah's death order once he carried it to the battlefield, we sign and seal verbal and emotional attacks with unrestrained comments and criticism. Once unleashed, we cannot totally undo them. Even unrestrained flattery can come back to haunt us; to encourage someone beyond their gifting and capability is hazardous. As leaders we must strategically and thoughtfully offer truth, mixed with the unmatched gift of timing, to those God has trusted us with in our environment.

RESTRAIN YOURSELF!

Restraint means neither bragging nor demeaning oneself. This is more difficult than it at first may seem. Too often we are quick to toot our own horns, letting others know where our strengths lie. Often this behavior is rooted in insecurity and fear. Insecurity that if we aren't intentional about making others aware of our individual and unique strengths and gifts, they will not notice them on their own. Fear comes into play when we think that this supposed passing over of our gifts and talents will steal from us potential opportunities that might otherwise be available.

On the flip side, many have substituted the desired characteristic of humility for an inability to accept a compliment or acknowledge one's own strengths or gifts. When offered a compliment or recognition for a job well done, these individuals are quick to invalidate what has been offered with self-denigrating denial. This behavior is indicative of a lack of self-restraint rooted in fear and insecurity. Fear that if one acknowledges the strengths recognized by others, that they will be perceived as being prideful or haughty. Insecurity based in what others might think or feel about them if this were so. The funny thing is that fear of what others will think is essentially rooted in pride.

Our primary goal in every area of our lives should be to please and honor the Lord. When we shift our focus from man-pleasing to God-pleasing, several things happen:

First, we will stop concentrating on what others think of us all the time. When our focus is consistently toward what the Lord thinks of us, we can be assured that both our words and actions will show self-restraint.

Second, the acknowledgement of our own strengths and gifts will become an opportunity to be thankful to the Lord. We know that anything good that comes from us was placed within us by our Creator. Therefore, when we humbly receive recognition or honor for a job well done, in doing so we are glorifying the Lord for what He has enabled us to do. To tritely dismiss recognition is to deny ourselves an opportunity to remember the goodness of God working through us, even though we are completely flawed and incapable of doing *good* in our own strength.

Finally, when shifting from a man-pleasing focus to a God-pleasing focus, the need to exalt ourselves is removed because this paradigm shift positions us to trust. When we acknowledge that all productivity that comes from us originates with Him, we can be confident that as we honor Him with our lives, He will utilize what He has placed within us to its utmost potential.

Restraint will change the way we think — and talk. It strengthens us not to chime in when the talk in the break room is not edifying, or perhaps even accurate. Ephesians 4:29 (ESV) exhorts us, "Let no corrupting talk come out of your mouths, but only such as is good for building up, as fits the occasion, that it may give grace to those who hear." So there is the measuring stick: if what comes out of your mouth isn't imparting grace to those who hear it, then perhaps more self-restraint is in order.

The ultimate example of restraint was demonstrated many times as Jesus lived His life on earth. Not succumbing to the temptations of Satan in the wilderness. Not destroying those who sought to torture and crucify Him. He knew when to reach out and speak out; He knew when to withdraw at the perfect time. He did not do anything that He didn't see the Father doing. And everything He did glorified His Father.

THE IT FACTOR

■ RESTRAINT

Post a guard at my mouth, God, set a watch at the door of my lips. Don't let me so much as dream of evil or thoughtlessly fall into bad company. (Psalm 141:3–4 *The Message*)

A quick response can ruin everything.

- Restraint means to hold back our words, take time to think before we speak, and consider how to best deliver what we have to say.
- It is impossible to retract words once they are spoken but it *is* possible to stop the words before we allow them to come out of our mouths.

- One of the biggest challenges regarding restraint is remembering we do not have to communicate everything that comes to our minds.

- Gossiping and spreading rumors creates rifts in our relationships, detracts from our credibility and causes others not to trust us. While it is good to be friendly and sociable, we must actively discipline our tongues when it comes to bragging, exaggerating, or talking about others. Proverbs 25:9–10 (NLT) warns us: *"When arguing with your neighbor, don't betray another person's secret. Others may accuse you of gossip, and you will never regain your good reputation."*

- Words have power that can bury dreams, demolish self-esteem, and destroy potential. Many times we point out the faults and bad habits of people, but fail to recognize and express their talents and potential. Words also have the power to build people up, set dreams to flight and inspire hope.

- Words can bring solutions or tie us to problems.

- How we speak is just as important as *what* we say. The tone, expression and attitude in which we convey our thoughts speak volumes and have tremendous impact on the listener.

> *There are going to be times when people wrong us. We need to show wisdom and restraint in how we confront them. Attempting to resolve a problem or bring clarification is good. Retaliation, however, is not what God wants from us. Motive is everything. As Romans 12:17–19 (The Message) says: Don't hit back; discover beauty in everyone. If you've got it in you, get along with everybody. Don't insist on getting even; that's not for you to do. "I'll do the judging," says God. "I'll take care of it."*

■ QUESTION

Which aspect of restraint presents the biggest challenge to you: stopping yourself before you say or do hurtful things, taking part in gossip, exaggeration or bragging, or taking the initiative to build others up?

■ BENEFITS OF RESTRAINT

You will reap many benefits from practicing restraint:

- When you control the impulsiveness of your words, you eliminate the regret that comes after saying something wrong.

> *Wise words satisfy like a good meal; the right words bring satisfaction. The tongue can bring death or life; those who love to talk will reap the consequences*
> (Proverbs 18:20–21 NLT).

- Others will trust you and be open to your opinions because you have established credibility by avoiding idle and destructive talk.
- Restraint helps you grow in your ability to analyze. When you learn to think things through, it makes you a good listener and you gain insight into people and situations. You can use this insight to form better answers and to speak so that others can hear you.
- The right words at the right time can breathe life and energy into a person like nothing else.

> *The wise in heart are called prudent, understanding, and knowing, and winsome speech increases learning [in both speaker and listener]. Understanding is a wellspring of life to those who have it, but to give instruction to fools is folly. The mind of the wise instructs his mouth, and adds*

learning and persuasiveness to his lips. Pleasant words
are as a honeycomb, sweet to the mind and healing to
the body (Proverbs 16:21–24 AMP).

Which benefit would you most desire to have? How do you see that benefit making a difference your life?

■ CHARACTERISTICS OF RESTRAINT

When people exemplify restraint:

- They are consistent and keep their integrity intact. Those with integrity have a unity of thought, word, and action. They realize that others will interpret what their convictions, values, and beliefs are by what they say and how they say it.
- They think before they speak. They do not have outbursts or talk over others. They recognize that their words are an expression of who they are and who God is, so they choose them carefully.

A gentle answer deflects anger, but harsh words make
tempers flare. The tongue of the wise makes knowledge
appealing, but the mouth of a fool belches out foolish-
ness. The LORD *is watching everywhere, keeping his eye*
on both the evil and the good. Gentle words are a tree
of life; a deceitful tongue crushes the spirit (Proverbs
15:1–4 NLT).

- They are good listeners. They analyze what they hear and choose their response based on the best way to communicate to the other person.
- They look for opportunities to lift others up and encourage them.

- They maintain an attitude that is geared to bring help and healing to others rather than an attitude that is condescending, dismissive, or aggressive.

■ QUESTION:

Do you know someone who demonstrates restraint? What do you admire about that person? What must you do to be more like him or her?

■ RESTRAINT STEPS TO FOLLOW

Read the steps to follow below and use them to develop a specific measurable action step to take this week.

1. Consistently take a moment to think before you speak. Your words have power. Use your power wisely. Proverbs 29:20 (*The Message*; author's emphasis) encourages us in this way: Observe the people who always talk *before* they think — even simpletons are better off than they are.

2. Recognize the power of the right words at the right time. Congratulate others and encourage them. On many occasions this could transform lives and circumstances and change destiny. If you feel you need to offer some correction or advice, choose your moment wisely so that the other person is in the right frame of mind to receive your words and your intent behind them. "Timely advice is lovely, like golden apples in a silver basket" (Proverbs 25:11 NLT).

3. When in a conflict with someone, write down the things you want to say. You will then have the opportunity to evaluate, correct, and polish your words. This will help you to keep your thoughts straight and prevent you from giving responses based on emotion and the heat of the moment.

4. Work on staying calm. When you feel negative emotion start to well up, take a deep breath and give yourself a few seconds before you respond. If you still feel the urge to speak in haste, ask a clarifying question instead.

5. Be aware of your tone, the words you use and your body language. How you say something is just as important as what you say.

6. Listen to understand rather than listening to respond. When someone else is speaking, stop yourself from coming up with your next argument. This is part of understanding people, but it also requires restraint. Our pride wants us to be thinking on our feet so we can one-up the other person with our rebuttal. We have to set aside our ego when we are showing godly restraint.

> *Pride first, then the crash, but humility is precursor to honor.*
> *Answering before listening is both stupid and rude*
> (Proverbs 18:12–13 *The Message*).

7. Don't forget to use restraint at home. Sometimes, when we are at home, we just let it all out and our families are the recipient of everything we have been holding back. That is not fair to the ones we love. Proverbs 25:24 (AMP) says: "It is better to dwell in the corner of the housetop than to share a house with a disagreeing, quarrelsome, *and* scolding woman." Do not cause your family to regret being related to you. If you feel like you are going to explode, find a way to release the tension without blowing it out on the ones you love. Talk to your spouse or a friend about what is troubling you, spend some time reading the Word or in prayer, or give yourself some time to worship and allow the Lord to quiet your Spirit and reassure you that He is in control.

Watch your words and hold your tongue; you'll save yourself a lot of grief (Proverbs 21:23 *The Message*).

Share your specific action step. Remember to keep it specific by attaching a who, what, where or when to the statement.

_____

_____

_____

_____

_____

_____

_____

_____

_____

_____

_____

_____

_____

_____

_____

_____

_____

_____

CHAPTER 7

THE VALUE OF HONESTY

The Proverbs 31 woman could certainly be characterized as honest. The fact that her husband fully depended on her to do him only good and not harm (31:11–12) implies that she was trustworthy — an honest person.

There is more than one aspect to honesty. Another aspect involves being honest with ourselves. The Proverbs 31 woman also seems to have done that. She's an evaluator, a person who makes conscious choices when she sees needs and is honest enough with herself to admit that she's not required to do it all. By having servants in her household, it's obvious she knew she couldn't do it all.

Let's consider a possible scenario. One of the helpers she has in the household is an incredible cook. She can make pastries that kick up any Bethlehem ladies' brunch. Our heroine can roast a lamb like nobody's business, but the sweets just aren't her gift. So, common sense would have her say to herself, "I'll roast the lamb, and my helper can do the pastry."

Whether we're in the kitchen, church choir loft, or the boardroom — God calls us to be honest with ourselves about what He's placed within us. Honesty isn't settling for *less*; it's making ourselves available for *more*. Honesty breeds success when you use what you have to accomplish the God-dream inside of you.

131

Perhaps you are coming out of a season where you tried to be something you weren't. You failed and now the enemy has stolen every last ounce of motivation from you. Isn't it interesting how silly we feel when God shows us that we've been lying to ourselves? He's had to allow a failure to lovingly move us along in the journey toward our original calling and purpose. When we settle for less than what God intends for us, we settle for less than His best.

Honesty with ourselves is a primary conduit to continued growth in life. Those who are willing to be honest with themselves are able to see, accept, and work on areas of weakness. This ability is critical to the continued spiritual journey of being taken from glory to glory.

Individuals are confronted with truth from God's Word by the Holy Spirit, as well as by those who live and work around them. When confronted with difficult truth about themselves, people typically respond a variety of ways. Some, like the fairy-tale gingerbread man "run, run, run as fast as they can" in the other direction. Healthier individuals submit to the reality that to live fully is to embrace ourselves and deal with our issues — because we all have them.

The person we lie to most often is the one we see in the mirror every morning. How many times have we said, "I'm fine, everything is all right" when all the while we are hurting on the inside, filled with fear, or ready to give in to defeat? The more we attempt to cover up with a facade we have created to protect our pride, the more into bondage we fall. By attempting to fix it ourselves or by ignoring whatever the issue is, we continue to lie to ourselves and make it impossible to find freedom.

Jesus, the light of all men, longs to shed His light into our hearts, not to condemn us but to set us free. Only He truly knows our hearts and what lies within them. Always a gentleman, He waits for permission to shed His light in those dark places where truth is needed. Truth that brings freedom.

HEARING THE TRUTH

We all have that friend. The one who we call when we really want the truth in a matter. The one we know will not lie to us in order to spare our feelings but will be quick to hand us a tissue when we cry. The one who will confirm the truth that already lives within us and draw it out with love-filled confrontation.

We also know those who will listen and simply agree with whatever you say. These are friends who are more than happy to start up where you leave off when grumbling or complaining. They feed the fire of your emotions by bringing the balloons to your pity party and stroking your ego, even when you are in the wrong. These friends will flatter you rather than point out where you have faltered. And they will say what they think you want to hear because they would rather stay in your good graces than risk potential conflict. After all, bearing the brunt of truth can be a heavy burden. These types of friends are not the ones we call when we want truth. They are the ones we call when we want to whine or feel sorry for ourselves, or when we are just looking for a sympathetic ear.

When we really want the truth though and are ready for change, we call *that* friend. Yep, you know the one. The friend that tells us, "Yes, those pants do make you look fat." The friend that tells us to stop whining, pick ourselves up, and get moving. The friend that helps us grow and change ourselves for the better to become the person God intended us to be. The Word of God tells us, "You will know the truth and the truth will set you free" (John 8:32). There is freedom found in the truth that can be found nowhere else. They know that what they say may hurt our feelings or make us mad, but they also love us enough to take that risk.

These are the very friends that, after they hear the depths of our heart on a matter, have the courage to say, "You're wrong and this is why." These are the friends that will point out where we have erred and then pray for us and with us, asking God for the wisdom and courage to know how to handle the situation in a way that honors Him. These are the friends who, as they are speaking truth, that very truth is confirmed within our hearts by the Spirit of God. Everyone should be blessed enough to have at least one of these friends.

Being completely honest with others involves risk: the risk of being judged unfairly, the risk of rejection, or the risk of losing face. When we are bound to the worry about pleasing others, the thought of laying down our pride stings too deeply. It can cause us to become slaves to that fear and stay forever bound to those lies. When we are honest with others, we show that our self-worth and confidence is not tied to their approval or their acceptance. When we are honest, we show ourselves to be a person of both integrity and confidence.

Honesty is tangible evidence that an individual has put more value in the Lord's opinion than that of others. Paul wrote in Galatians 1:10 (ESV): "For am I now seeking the approval of man, or of God? Or am I trying to please man? If I were still trying to please man, I would not be a servant of Christ." In this Scripture, Paul makes it clear that if our focus is on being pleasing to God, we will not always be pleasing to people. It all boils down to where our priorities lie. Is it the desire of your heart to be a pleaser of man or a pleaser of God? If your answer is to be a pleaser of God, then you can know that desire is always achieved if we are completely honest in all matters of life. For the Lord, this is a place of no compromise.

A famous preacher once said, "Truth is like medicine, it's hard to take but good for you." God tells us His Word is truth, and there is no better medicine than the words of our heavenly Father. Hearing the truth, speaking the truth, and walking in the truth may not always be easy, but we can be assured that it is the manner of living which will ultimately bring the most joy, peace, and prosperity.

SPEAKING THE TRUTH

Scripture tells us, "The tongue has the power of life and death, and those who love it will eat its fruit" (Proverbs 18:21). When we choose to honor the Lord by speaking words of truth, we open the door for good fruit to abound in our lives.

With our employees, if we have a track record of speaking truth, we become trustworthy in their eyes. Employees who view us as honest and trustworthy will feel comfortable working hard for the greater good of the company. Those who believe we will always tell them the truth will not doubt the motives of our heart or our level of integrity when difficult situations arise in which our leadership position demands we make hard choices that affect the company.

It is not only important how we speak *to* others; it is important how we speak *about* them. Most bosses have a boss, so it is crucial that those we lead in business see us model acceptance of others in their positions of authority. It is unrealistic that we should expect the respect of others when we are not willing to give that same respect to those in authority over us.

How often do we see women (and I know men do it too, but there's a specific female take on this) harshly criticize those in authority over them (when they're in places they aren't likely to be overheard) but then kiss up to those same people at the office? Is it honest to stab and kiss the same person? Sounds kind of like Judas to me. Is it honest to be kind to others only because we know they have something we need or want? This happens repeatedly in all walks of life but may be the most noticeable in business.

Because subtle forms of dishonesty sneak into our lives, often without us realizing it, we must allow the Lord to shine His light of truth into our hearts on a daily basis and ask that He seek out these subtle deceptions, reveal them to us, and help us to walk in a manner that is worthy of our calling (Colossians 1:10).

The words we speak are like seeds. These seeds can be planted in the hearts of others as well as into our own. When we lie, pervert the truth, or give half-truths, we are planting seeds that produce rotten fruit. Imagine a garden sown with corrupted seeds; the fruit that would be produced would also be corrupted. This problem is then compounded because the seeds that are produced from the harvest would only produce more corruption. And so the cycle continues; corruption breeds more corruption just as lies produce more lies. The opposite is also true. When we sow words of integrity, we reap integrity, both in our own life and in the lives of others. Seeds of honesty produce the kind of fruit that we desire in our lives.

In our tech-savvy world, our words are no longer just spoken. Are we still acting honestly when our fingers are flying over a keyboard emailing or texting? I ask myself this when I choose to hit "Like" on Facebook: *Do I really "like" the idea or statement presented? Or do I see it as agreeing in order to feel like part of the crowd?* The inclusiveness of social media helps us to feel close to others in an artificial way. Of the people who state "praying" in that venue, I wonder how many are actually praying? It's so easy to throw out the words "I'll pray for you" at the conclusion of a conversation where hurts or difficulties have been shared. Often however, as soon as we leave that social media site, that person's prayer needs disappear into the abyss of our ever-busy lives. It is not that our heart isn't for them. Our best intentions are indeed to pray for them. Unfortunately, our intentions many times do not match up with our actions.

It's better to stop right in the midst of a conversation when a need is mentioned and pray for that person, rather than to be dishonest and never follow through on our words. An idle word is one we speak which has no purpose. A promise to pray for someone without follow-through is an idle word at its worst.

WALKING IN THE TRUTH

Although honest words are important, the apostle John reminded us that there is something more important:

> *Dear children, let us not love with words or speech but with actions and in truth. This is how we know that we belong to the truth and how we set our hearts at rest in his presence: If our hearts condemn us, we know that God is greater than our hearts, and he knows everything* (1 John 3:18–20).

More often than not, we are our own worst enemy when it comes to acting on the truth. If we know what God's Word says, and intentionally disobey it, we will feel convicted. This is true if we are still tenderhearted enough to sense the grief of the Holy Spirit in a sin area we need to address. However, continual disobedience does have the ability to lead to a place of hard-heartedness. Ezekiel pointed out that God had to do a type of spiritual heart surgery on the people of his day: "I will give you a new heart and put a new spirit in you; I will remove from you your heart of stone and give you a heart of flesh" (Ezekiel 36:26).

Not only does our disobedience bring conviction, it can also bring distance from God in the love relationship that is His ultimate desire for us. A love relationship of intimacy is, in His heart, far above all the *doing* which many equate with the Christian life. Our actions are no doubt important as a gauge of our dedication to the Lord, for as the Word reminds us in James 2:17 (ESV), "faith by itself, if it does not have works, is dead."

Outward actions of devotion, however, are never to become *idols of habit*. In other words, we must not let our church attendance or missions work or charitable acts become a substitute for other, less visible acts of devotion in the Christian life. Just going through the motions is not what God's heart is seeking. In fact, that kind of empty religious behavior is, throughout His Word condemned as detestable. If it's just an act with no meaning, He makes it clear that He would rather have nothing.

We may look at actions as simply an outward thing, but the humbling thing is God knows our every *intention*. First Samuel 16:7 tells us that man looks on the outward appearance, but the Lord looks at the heart. Regardless of how good our actions may seem, if the motives behind them are not pure before the Lord, in His eyes our actions will have no value.

The challenge to "do nothing out of selfish ambition or vain conceit" (Philippians 2:3) is a tall order in a society where self-management and vocational drive are almost worshipped. How often are our actions motivated by the desire to impress others or at least to avoid their judgment? There is an unfortunate payday for those who plan their actions based solely on pleasing others or gaining acceptance. Those actions will lead to burnout and sometimes bitterness. Deceitfulness will eventually be uncovered. Perhaps others won't discover our wrong motives, but the emptiness of walking

away from God's dream for us — because it doesn't seem as big as our
dream — will leave a broken heart behind.

> *My late mom-in-law's Bible is an absolute treasure that*
> *my sisters-in-law gifted to me after Mary went to be with*
> *the Lord in 2006. One morning, as I was seeking God in*
> *His Word, there was in her handwriting a note on a page.*
> *It said, "What I leave in my children is more important*
> *than what I leave to my children."*

How often do we see heirs to a financial windfall squander it away
or lavishly invest in their own demise through loving money and
its power more than the relationships around them? More than an
inheritance of wealth, parents who really love their children desire
to leave them a legacy of a life lived honestly before the Lord. A life
which exemplifies honesty in their words and in their dealings with
others.

A WOMAN OF DECEPTION

Honesty, in a person or in a corporation, is hard to come by, but it's
not a new problem. In Acts 5 we read the story of Ananias and his wife,
Sapphira. In those days of the early church, believers lived much more
communally than at any other time in history. Often they would pool
their resources. As the story begins, Barnabas had just sold a field he
owned and had given all the proceeds to the apostles for the needs of
the church (Acts 4:36–37). In the way of churches, then and now, the
public gift and Barnabas' generosity were probably widely discussed.

Ananias and Sapphira had certainly heard about the gift and had
seen how admired Barnabas was because of it. The couple also had

a piece of property which they sold about that time. They may have genuinely cared about the needs of the church's people, but they also wanted to keep some of the money. Ananias devised a plan: "with his wife's full knowledge he kept back part of the money for himself, but brought the rest and put it at the apostles' feet." By making the gift the same way Barnabas did, they wanted everyone to believe they were giving all the money. They even wanted double acclaim because they planned for Ananias to make the gift alone and then several hours later Sapphira would show up so that everyone could ooh and aah over her. (That sounds more like it would have been Sapphira's idea, doesn't it?) But plans have a way of going awry.

It was an act of free will, an offering under no duress. In the process of selling their land and turning a profit, they had every right to keep some or all of the compensation for themselves. The problem didn't come into play until they decided to feign the amount they were offering as the total price of the land. Through the insight God gave him, Peter immediately saw what was being done and confronted Ananias.

> *Then Peter said, "Ananias, how is it that Satan has so filled your heart that you have lied to the Holy Spirit and have kept for yourself some of the money you received for the land? Didn't it belong to you before it was sold? And after it was sold, wasn't the money at your disposal? What made you think of doing such a thing? You have not lied just to human beings but to God"* (Acts 5:3–4).

Stricken with the truth and his sin, Ananias fell over dead and was carried out. Sapphira, not knowing what had happened to her husband, showed up three hours later. Peter gave her the chance to tell the truth by asking her if what they had brought was the full price of the land. When she lied and said it was, he told her that the same young men who buried her husband would also carry her out. She fell down dead.

Because of the dishonesty of this couple and what happened to them, great fear fell on the church. It was a significant message to those believers — if you choose to lie to the Holy Spirit, there is a great price to pay. It's just not worth it.

HONESTY WITH GOD

Isn't it laughable that we would try to fool God? Either with our words or with our actions? When we try to fool God what we really do is lengthen our journey to freedom. Ultimately, if we refuse to be honest with the Lord, like Ananias and Sapphira, we cause our own death — emotionally, mentally, and perhaps even physically.

I always think of Peter and his denial when I review my own honesty with God and those times I've promised Him I'd do everything He asked or that I'd never fall into a certain sin again, etc. I'm ashamed to think of the times that I've been lulled into deception, complacency, or just outright disobedience. Imagine the incredible pain in Peter's spirit when he heard that rooster crowing and realized that, just as Jesus predicted, he had denied Him three times. It actually brings a wave of nausea just thinking about it. *What if that was me? What would I do if Jesus were looking me in the eye and saw I had just betrayed Him?* What a horrible, wretched feeling! There's no escape from the Holy Spirit's blade of conviction cutting into the depths of our hearts.

When we look at the last chapter of the Gospel of John, we see Peter again, joyous and thankful to see Jesus on the shore. However, like me, Peter's kind of a jerk. When he gets the opportunity to speak with Jesus, he starts comparing himself with another disciple (John 21:20–22). There you go — back into the muck of self-unrealization. He's not able to see that what God has for him is uniquely his own mission. Like many of us.

How long will it take the majority of women who are Christ followers to stop asking, "What about her — why does she get to stay home with her kids full time?" Or, "Why do I have to give up what I'm best at? Is it wrong for me to love my career?" Haven't you heard the questions? Perhaps from a friend or even milling around in your own head?

When Jesus asks, "Do you love Me?" do you say, "Yes, Lord, *but* — "

Do you love Him enough to trust Him? If you are called to be at home, do you love Jesus enough to believe that if He's called you to be there, He will make a way? Do you as a corporate executive, schoolteacher, doctor, retail clerk, or food-service worker love Jesus enough to believe that He can use you in your vocation? Can you sense His presence living through you to change the hearts, minds, and futures of people you connect with in the environment in which He has placed you?

God's heart is full of compassion for us as He sees the way our lives are destroyed by our unwillingness to be honest with ourselves, others, and Him. For some reason we deceive ourselves into thinking that we can fool Him and that our dishonesty will not be discovered. Wrong! When we are honest with God, we give Him permission to shine all of who He is into every area of our lives, bringing freedom into those places. Many are afraid to be truly honest with Him because they fear rejection — even though intellectually they know that He already knows everything about them.

Think of it this way: What doctor can heal a wound he isn't given access to? God is called the Great Physician, and the perfect love that drives out fear described in 1 John 4:18 is the medicine He uses to heal us. This perfect love drives out all fear of judgment, rejection, or abandonment. This perfect love allows us to stand naked both emotionally and mentally in front of our Creator and to allow ourselves to be embraced just as we are. It doesn't get much more honest than that.

THE IT FACTOR

■ HONESTY

What this adds up to, then, is this: no more lies, no more pretense. Tell your neighbor the truth. In Christ's body we're all connected to each other, after all. When you lie to others, you end up lying to yourself. (Ephesians 4:25 *The Message*)

Telling lies will get you in trouble, but honesty is its own defense.

- Honesty is a direct reflection of your inner character and helps to create a sure foundation for healthy relationships. Reflecting God's truth in our words and actions is part of introducing others to Him. Colossians 3:9–10 urges us: "Do not lie to each other, since you have taken off your old self with its practices and have put on the new self, which is being renewed in knowledge in the image of its Creator."

- When we communicate honestly, we are open and upfront and refuse to falsify information or manipulate the truth. Honest people display fairness and equality in what they say and how they behave. If we are honest, we do not lie, cheat, or steal.

- Honesty is rooted in our motives and intents. A statement can be literally true but still dishonest if the intention is to deceive or manipulate rather than being transparent and truthful.

- Telling the *whole truth* is an important part of honesty. When we tell *the whole truth,* we do not omit any relevant details or information in order to mislead or misrepresent the facts. Leaving out some of the truth is usually an attempt to manipulate the situation. "Whoever speaks the truth gives honest evidence, but a false witness utters deceit" (Proverbs 12:17 ESV).

- If everyone were honest, the world would be a much nicer and easier place in which to live:

  1. We would not need to lock our doors or have walls or fences around our property.

  2. The need for police and prisons would decrease because a large portion of our crime is the result of lying, cheating, and stealing.

  3. The divorce rate would likely be reduced because people would not consider unfaithfulness an option. They would choose to work on their relationships instead.

  4. There would be less need for attorneys. The courts and taxpayers would be free from the cost of frivolous lawsuits.

  5. Businesses would run more efficiently. There would be less time involved in getting to the truth of a conflict, people would take responsibility for their workload, and they would be honest with the resources entrusted to them. Proverbs 16:11 (*The Message*): God cares about honesty in the workplace; your business is his business.

- Honesty requires courage. Telling the truth can be uncomfortable, especially when it produces pain for ourselves or conflict with others.

- Being honest takes work and intentionality. It can be easy to fall into the lying trap. There will be times that we face difficult situations and will need to work to keep our eyes on God in order to find the answers.

- Dishonesty will bankrupt a person. It will rob you of your reputation, your respect, your resources, and your influence.

■ QUESTION

When is it most difficult to be honest? Do you ever struggle with being truthful with yourself?

■ BENEFITS OF HONESTY

If you are an honest person, you will experience the following benefits:

- You will be known and respected as a person of integrity. People will trust what you say and expect the best from you.
- You will have a clear conscience. You will be at peace with others and with God. You will feel good about your actions and decisions. You will not experience the guilt that comes from being dishonest or the worry which results from fearing your lies will be uncovered. "God can't stomach liars; he loves the company of those who keep their word" (Proverbs 12:22 *The Message*).
- Your opinions will have weight and your words will hold influence because people have confidence in you and trust you to be fair and not play favorites.
- Your relationships will be strong because they are built on trust.
- People will depend on you. When people see they can trust you with small things, they will begin to trust you with bigger things.

> *Who may ascend the mountain of the Lord? Who may stand in his holy place? The one who has clean hands and a pure heart, who does not trust in an idol or swear by a false god. They will receive blessing from the Lord and vindication from God their Savior* (Psalm 24:3–5).

Which benefit would you most desire to have? How do you see that benefit making a difference your life?

■ CHARACTERISTICS OF HONESTY

When people exemplify honesty:

- They tell the *whole truth* even when it is not convenient or puts them at a disadvantage. They are credible and maintain a good reputation.
- They are genuine and transparent. They do not skip over portions of the truth or twist meanings to benefit themselves or manipulate others.
- They are fair, try to do right by others, and only keep that which belongs to them. They do not lie, cheat, or steal to get ahead and they return items that are not theirs. They take the words of Deuteronomy 25:13–16 (*The Message*) to heart:

> *Don't carry around with you two weights, one heavy and the other light, and don't keep two measures at hand, one large and the other small. Use only one weight, a true and honest weight, and one measure, a true and honest measure, so that you will live a long time on the land that God, your God, is giving you. Dishonest weights and measures are an abomination to God, your God — all this corruption in business deals!*

- They take responsibility for their decisions and are good stewards of the resources provided to them. This includes their time and talents as well as responsibilities and property that others entrust to them.
- They know how to distinguish the truth from a lie. They are self-aware and do not lie to themselves. They know how to differentiate between that which they wish to be true and that which is true.

■ QUESTION

Do you know someone you consider to be very honest? What do you admire about that person? What must you do to be more like him or her?

■ HONESTY STEPS TO FOLLOW

Read the steps to follow below and use them to develop a specific measurable action step to take this week.

1. **Make a commitment to tell the truth.** Honor your commitment by being honest in everything and with everyone. Tell the truth even when it hurts or is connected to negative consequences. You and your reputation will be better for it.

2. **Consider your words before you speak them.** Be aware of what the *whole truth* is before you give an answer. Do not hold back on the truth because you want to please everyone.

3. **Identify your motives before you speak and be kind.** When honestly delivering a tough message, be careful to speak out of concern rather than to put someone in their place. Being more hurtful in your honesty than necessary will result in alienating those you should be trying to help.

4. **Conduct yourself with integrity.** Be careful not to twist the truth or leave part of the story out in order to manipulate a person or situation.

5. **Speak up when you know that something must be said.** Be aware that sometimes keeping silent is dishonesty. If you know about a lie and keep quiet, the lie lives on.

6. **Do not allow yourself to get caught up in "little white lies."** Avoid taking part in cover-ups or lying for the sake of convenience, even in situations where it seems easier to cover up what really happened.

The answer's simple: Live right, speak the truth, despise exploitation, refuse bribes, reject violence, avoid evil amusements. This is how you raise your standard of living! A safe and stable way to live. A nourishing, satisfying way to live (Isaiah 33:15–16 *The Message*).

Share your specific action step. Remember to keep it specific by attaching a who, what, where, or when to the statement.

_____

_____

_____

_____

_____

_____

_____

_____

_____

_____

_____

_____

_____

_____

_____

_____

_____

_____

CHAPTER 8

The Value of Planning

The Proverbs 31 woman was a good planner. I'm not saying that she had a hot pink three-ring binder filled with household hints for stain removal and hummus recipes. Rather, she saw the needs of the day, month, year, and season and planned accordingly. Along the way, however, she displayed the skill of being flexible enough to adjust to accomplish a new task without getting uptight because, "it wasn't on my list for today."

Verse 13 tells us "she selects wool and flax and works with eager hands." Selecting takes time. She planned time out of her schedule to find the things she needed to be productive. It wasn't that she didn't have other things to do. Quite the contrary, what we read about her schedule implies that she had *a lot* on her proverbial plate. But she found value in the ability to work with her hands and planned accordingly so that she would have something to work with. Her actions remind us that planning leads to productivity.

"She gets up while it is still night; she provides food for her family and portions for her female servants." This woman planned her day to meet the needs of those in her care before she did other things. She had her priorities in order and got up as early as necessary to get them done. Before planning what she *wanted* to do, she planned what she *needed* to do.

In verse 21 we are told that she isn't afraid of the snow because her family is clothed well. When we are wise in our planning, there is less room for fear to take root. Second Timothy 1:7 (NLT) tells us that God has not given us a spirit of fear, but one of "power, love, and self-discipline." Many times, poor planning unintentionally invites fear into our lives, stealing both productivity and joy in the process. If we plan our budget well, we will not fear that we won't be able to meet all our financial obligations. If we plan our staff well, we will not fear that a decision they make will poorly impact our company.

Even when her entrepreneurial sensibilities took over, for example seeing a field and buying it, the Proverbs 31 woman knew how to plan for the unexpected. Her forethought made it possible for her to take advantage of unforeseen opportunities. Evidently she had planned well enough to save some money, which her husband gave her liberty to use according to her own vision. Credit lines and the like were not available to the small businesswoman of Bible times. Therefore, she had to be very wise with how she handled her finances.

Her ability to plan well was used by God to bless many — her family as she brought honor to it and some community members who were provided with consistent employment. She was blessed to be able to be a blessing.

PLAN TO BE FLEXIBLE

Planning is required in every area of life. From the smallest things to the greatest, to at least some degree, "failing to plan is planning to fail." In fact, planning is such a crucial part of our lives that often we do it automatically. Planning our grocery shopping around the meals we will eat that week. Planning our budget so that we have sufficient funds to meet our needs and desires. Planning our schedule so that we are able to live a balanced life, one which enables us to divide our time appropriately between various tasks and obligations.

Some people are not list makers but have an almost innate sense of how and when things should be done, gleaned from good habits of observation and discernment. Others feel they must write everything down and mark things off their lists to avoid challenges developing into crises. Regardless of what it looks like, planning is essential to our well-being and productivity.

I (Lisa) am not, by nature, a planner in the traditional sense. Instead, I tend to be a big-picture person, really preferring to leap right into the completed and functioning vision that I see in my mind's eye. Dawn, on the other hand, plans strategically and embraces a systems philosophy. The daily demands we face within our individual work environments are quite different.

A specialty-food business environment is tied to health regulations and structure (following recipes, for instance), but there's also something adventurous and flexible about food creation. A recipe modification might be required, even in the context of formulated procedures. It's much like music, art, or a creative process of any kind. There is still a freedom that is an essential element. For a noncommodity offering, things are always subject to change.

The opposite is true with the technical installation business that Dawn's family has been proficient at for decades. There is a specific beginning and end, and success is identified with training technicians to make all of the proper connections in between. In that business there is definitely a right and wrong way to do things and not much flexibility.

As different as these industries may appear, they, as well as every other proficient business are successful because they are based on planning. So it is with families, churches — and yes, even one-on-one relationships.

Some couples say they couldn't have a healthy relationship without a planned date night. Their lifestyles require they must literally schedule time together. This can especially be important in dual-earner families with children and, specifically, in certain seasons of life. Responsibility, work, and family tasks can steal valuable quality time that is necessary for the maintenance of a healthy and intimate relationship between spouses. A failure to invest time and energy results in poor dividend returns — even relationally speaking.

Some people (such as the authors of this book) work together with their spouses. Lisa and Bob Troyer work together constantly and consistently interact throughout each day. For better or worse (remember those marriage vows?), this kind of up close and personal working relationship also requires a plan. Especially when working together, it is important to have times when it is agreed to step away and view life through a different lens than that of mutual work interests. (In other words, ban the business talk!) Dawn and her husband, Jeff, also work together. However, because of the structure of their company, it's not as mutually hands-on as it is with the Troyers.

What does this have to do with the value of planning? It appears that within every situation, there is a plan that brings success even if that plan has to be open and available to immediate change. For instance, the couple who is aware of the need to *plan* time to be together may have to become flexible in their perception of what a "date night" looks like. Sometimes a lack of time or financial resources may prevent them from spending a night out on the town or having a weekend away in the mountains. Instead, a few extra hours alone in bed on a Saturday morning (with the bedroom door locked) could serve the same purpose and meet the same relational needs a lot closer to home.

Flexibility within a plan is crucial. In fact, being prepared for your initial plan to encounter some bumps in the road can help you keep your cool when things don't turn out the way you initially expected.

These relational truths for couples apply to the relationships with other family members as well. We must be purposeful about planning and having intentional quality time with our children. We dare not neglect this despite the other demands of daily living. And as adult children, if our parents are still living and willing for us to help care for them in necessary ways, we honor both them and the Lord when we plan time to do so.

PLAN TO BE FINANCIALLY FREE

Our friend Beth is a planner. She's very intentional about her schedule, because with five children she realized long ago that she didn't have a choice if she wasn't going to live in perpetual chaos. As of this writing, her eldest is married to a wonderful young man who is serving in the military overseas. Her second is completing her master's degree while coaching basketball at the college level. Her middle child is in her freshman year of college, the fourth daughter is beginning her high school career and is an active athlete, and the "baby" is 12 and keeps his mother busy buying jeans with longer inseams.

Beth loves her husband and children, the Amish family for whom she helps with payroll duties for their thriving family business, and the elderly folks she visits weekly at the local retirement home for community prayer group. In addition, she tends to her mother's needs as she interacts with caregivers who tenderly care for her mom. In her late eighties, Beth's mom is now in need of constant care since having a stroke complicated by her Alzheimer's condition diagnosed about five years ago.

With such a full life, it would be incredibly easy to become encumbered, but Beth also is intentional about staying in God's Word. Beth has been my (Lisa's) accountability partner for over a decade. I have seen firsthand her attention to planning and the results of her Spirit-led life. During a very challenging season after the birth of her fifth child, Beth still scheduled accountability sessions with me and our two other group members. Being transparent, which was a focus of accountability, was a tool that God used to refine Beth's attitude toward difficult circumstances. This led to her ability to prayerfully confront issues of emotional detachment that were occurring within her marriage due to the *surprise* we now lovingly call Clay. She's the first to admit, it was a hard season, especially when one of her children was not thrilled to have a baby in the house.

Beth found that planning was required because there are times when we simply have no choice. But, even in the midst of emotional confusion, we can be equipped to sustain some stability if we do not neglect to plan to the degree that we are capable.

One of the reminders that helped Beth, and in turn those with whom she interacts, is a jar that contains walnuts and rice. Mine sits on my cupboard shelf as a treasured reminder to put first things first. The walnuts are our priorities: God, family, friends, work and self-care. The rice is the other stuff that occurs in everyone's life. The rice will fit around the walnuts in the jar. However, if we fill the jar completely with rice (stuff) — if we live "rice first" — there will be no room for the walnuts (priorities) in the jar. The simplicity of this physical illustration reminds us that unless we plan to address the priorities in our lives, other less significant things will usurp our time.

Another area in which Beth and her husband have experienced the benefits of planning is in their finances. She shares:

I believe a common myth about financial planning is that it is something only rich folks need to do. That thought could not be farther from the truth. That would be like saying only people who have a lot of kids need to be good parents. The amount has nothing to do with the goal. Parents of one child are just as concerned about their child being healthy in all areas of life as are those who have more than one. Likewise, the man who has $10 to spend in a day needs to be just as concerned about his financial plans as the one who has $100.

Some would say the man that has a lot does not need to plan at all, yet 1 Corinthians 4:2 (NKJV) states, *"Moreover it is required of stewards that one be found faithful."* It doesn't say stewards who are in charge of a little or a lot, it simply says stewards.

As followers of Christ, we are His stewards of all that has been entrusted to us: our time, our treasure, and our talents. In the Gospel of Luke, the good doctor reminds us that as stewards we are to take good care of what we tend to view as "ours," but it's not really ours, it's God's.

Financial planning is simply being aware of what you have and doing your best with it. When our best still doesn't seem good enough, we can count on God's Word for the next step. As with parenting, we do not always feel equipped to handle what has been entrusted to us. The answer to us in God's Word is always the same *"seek wise counsel."* If you don't know where to begin, start in Proverbs 1, and allow biblical truth to point you in the right direction. James 1:5 (NKJV) is also a reminder that, *"If any of you lacks wisdom, let him ask of God, who gives to all liberally and without reproach, and it will be given to him."*

The Bible is by far the best counsel in the area of stewardship. A basic Bible study on the subject will cover the ultimate goal in finances: stewardship. It also gives great advice as to the best means to attain financial goals. Proverbs 21:5 in *The Living Bible* states it quite simply, *"Steady plodding brings prosperity."* Steady plodding, one day, one dollar, one step at a time.

A good basic financial plan is the 10/10/80 plan. The first 10 percent is God's — giving back to God directs our attention and heart to Him. Matthew 6:21 (NKJV) tells us, *"For where your treasure is, there your heart will also be."* The next 10 percent is the steady plodding mentioned in Proverbs 21:5 — saving a little money today is the step to having more tomorrow. That is financial planning at the most basic level. It is not an unusual concept; the farmer plants a bag of seed in order to harvest a truckload of crops. No seed, no harvest. The same is true with saving. Unless there is an intentional planting of seed, there will be no harvest. The final 80 percent is ours to budget wisely in order to live within our means. A wise person once said, "If your outgo exceeds your income, your upkeep will be your downfall." In and out, up and down, it sounds like a balancing act because it is, and the first step to having a balanced budget is to have a budget in place.

Crown.org and daveramsey.com are two excellent online sources for biblical financial planning. Both offer online budgeting tools as well as individual or group study plans.

Financial planning is simply being intentional about having a plan in place in order to be a good steward of all that God has blessed us with.

— Beth

PLAN TO AVOID AN URGENCY EMERGENCY

Planning is essential for us to successfully handle things that we cannot afford to neglect. How many of us are always responding to the *urgent* because a crisis occurs (due to our lack of planning)? Or maybe it's just a *perceived* crisis? Every time you open your email, which messages do you see first? Those marked "urgent." However, urgent messages are only deemed so in the imagination of the one who is writing them. We need to ask God to help us determine in our jar of life's commitments if *the rice is crowding out the walnuts.* When our teens call us from school and cry "emergency," sometimes the best lesson we can teach them is that mom or dad will not always jump to their aid when they have forgotten projects or gym clothes. As one woman said her mother frequently told her, "Failure to plan on your part does not constitute an emergency on my part."

Helping our children, employees, and team members learn to plan wisely can enable them to avert disappointment and, perhaps, even disaster. If there's a red light flashing on your car's dashboard, then planning a visit to the local mechanic is the appropriate response. But, having regularly scheduled maintenance done might avoid the red light coming on.

We like the saying, "I don't know what I don't know." God doesn't usually lay out a blueprint of His plans for us to examine (or approve). We aren't responsible for what we don't or can't know. However, we are responsible for what we *do* know. Pleading ignorance is a deceitful habit many engage in to avoid accountability. Most people can see right through that excuse, and no one is served well by it.

PLAN TO FOLLOW YOUR VISION

Leaders must have an intentional plan to accomplish the needed duties of each day. They either need to take the responsibility to implement the plan personally or have others to whom they delegate.

The important thing is actually having a plan. Proverbs 29:18 tells us that without a vision, God's people perish. In Habakkuk 2:2–3 (NKJV) the Lord says:

> *Write the vision*
> *And make it plain on tablets,*
> *That he may run who reads it.*
> *For the vision is yet for an appointed time;*
> *But at the end it will speak, and it will not lie.*
> *Though it tarries, wait for it;*
> *Because it will surely come,*
> *It will not tarry.*

Planning helps to ensure the vision comes to pass. Writing the vision down helps to ensure that everyone involved (1) remains on the same page, and (2) can be reminded of the vision were they at some point to lose sight of it.

I have heard many in leadership roles of all sorts share that they have made a habit of being intentional about setting aside time for a "vision" or planning retreat annually. During this time, they purposefully remove themselves from familiar surroundings and get away for a time of prayer. Actually it sounds quite Jesus-esque as described in Luke 5:16. These leaders, seeking the Lord's plan for their life for the following year, open their spiritual ears and eyes to hear and see what the Lord has for them. Many write down what they believe the Lord has revealed to them so that they are able to remain focused on it for the rest of the year. This kind of intentionality, when feasible, can only be profitable. Proverbs 16:9 tells us that a man plans his way, but the Lord directs his steps. If we plan for our family, our business, or any other area of our lives without seeking the wisdom and direction of the Lord first, then we plan inefficiently and risk missing out on His best for us.

PLAN TO PRIORITIZE

Equally as important as having a vision is making that vision a part of your day by prioritizing. It is easy to get wrapped up in the right now rather than working a plan based on priorities. Because we both end up multitasking a lot, this is a struggle with which we both contend.

There is an old adage that if you don't plan your day, you become a part of someone else's plan. As we discussed in an earlier portion of the book, when you are one who takes responsibility, people will rely on you. This is a great benefit and brings great opportunity! But it can also make you a target for what we call "throwing a monkey on your back," which happens when someone is trying to get something off their to-do list by putting it on yours. This frees the original monkey carrier to pursue whatever they want — while *you* carry the burden of the monkey.

There are certain times and certain people that we should carry the monkey for, but we also need to know when to say enough. If our schedule becomes so crowded that we cannot carry out the vision God has given us, it is time to stop, rethink, and prayerfully consider our priorities.

By the same token, we can end up wasting our time when we do not have a plan. One thing I (Dawn) have found very helpful is using the Pareto Principle (also known as the 80/20 rule) in my daily planning. Whenever I do this, I find I become very productive and excited about what gets accomplished.

If you are not familiar with the Pareto Principle, it is an observation that Italian economist Vilfredo Pareto made in 1906 which stated that often 80 percent of the effect comes from 20 percent of the cause.

What this means in regard to planning is that 20 percent of our priorities will give us 80 percent of our production. To make our time productive, we need to turn that around and spend 80 percent of our time on that top 20 percent of our people and projects. Here is how I use Pareto's Principle to my benefit:

1. I first figure out my top 20 percent — the people who make a difference in my world and the projects that are high priority (like this book, for example).

2. I make a list of the things *I must do today* in order of importance. These are items that cannot be done by anyone but me and have a deadline.

3. I make a list of people I want to add value to by encouraging them or spending intentional development time with them. This is an important part of my every day. I do not want to lose any momentum on team-building because I know that what I invest today will have a return tomorrow.

4. I make a list of the things that need to be done but are not pressing. I then decide if I must be the one to do these or my time would be better spent delegating these to someone else.

5. I check the things off my list as they are accomplished and note the amount of time it took me to do each one.

This probably looks more clinical than spiritual, but I believe God is pleased when we use our resources well. And time is our most valuable resource.

PLAN TO GROW SPIRITUALLY

If we are not planning time in the Word of God, we will have little opportunity to influence anyone for His kingdom. Second Timothy

2:15 (NKJV) reminds us, "Be diligent to present yourself approved to God, a worker who does not need to be ashamed, rightly dividing the word of truth." In order to rightly divide the Word of Truth, we must plan to spend time studying and understanding it so that we are not only able to live it out ourselves, but present it to others with integrity.

We are encouraged in 1 Peter 3:15 (NKJV) to "always be ready to give a defense to everyone who asks you a reason for the hope that is in you, with meekness and fear." To always be ready involves planning ahead to fill yourself with the truth of God's Word so that you are always able to explain the source of your inner hope to others. Lack of planning in this area can greatly hinder our opportunity to be used by God as a messenger of reconciliation.

The importance of planning is evident in other places as well. If we don't plan to establish a tithing mentality, impulsive spending and selfishness will usurp our funds and impede our ability to help spread the gospel message to those around us.

There are many who constantly fail to accomplish what they know God has called them to do. This is unfortunate and happens for many reasons. Fear of failure, lack of faith, unwillingness to submit their own will to His will, and certainly lack of proper planning are only some of these reasons.

How many times have we longed to step out into a journey of faith, service, opportunity, for instance for a missions trip, but had to decline because our poor planning of time and resources left us with the inability to raise our hand and say, "Here I am, send (or spend) me"? We forget sometimes in life and in planning that our time here on the earth isn't really supposed to be about us at all. What it's really about is our part in helping the Lord accomplish *His* plan here through us. Matthew 5:16 (NKJV) exhorts us, "Let your light so shine before men, that they may see your good works and glorify your Father in heaven."

Our mutual goal, vision, and plan should be that our lives, in every way, would glorify the Father.

Do we fail in this occasionally? Of course. The grace of God is that He loves us and uses us anyway. However, when we give an account for our lives, will we be facing a Holy God with grief in our hearts because we missed out on His perfect will due to poor planning?

A WOMAN OF SUBSTANCE

Lydia was a woman of wisdom and business sense, a merchant, who didn't miss God's will for her life. We are introduced to her by Luke in Acts 16:13–15 (NKJV):

> And on the Sabbath day we went out of the city to the riverside, where prayer was customarily made; and we sat down and spoke to the women who met there. Now a certain woman named Lydia heard us. She was a seller of purple from the city of Thyatira, who worshiped God. The Lord opened her heart to heed the things spoken by Paul. And when she and her household were baptized, she begged us, saying, "If you have judged me to be faithful to the Lord, come to my house and stay." So she persuaded us.

Although the reference is short, it's obvious that Lydia's support of Paul's ministry was not only a blessing to him for immediate needs, but part of God's greater plan to reach women like you and me. This passage assures us that business women can be just as influential in the furtherance of the gospel as the dedicated Sunday School teacher. And, not only can they be just as influential, there are times when it is specifically the plan of God that they be utilized for service to His kingdom in this way.

Let's look a little closer at Lydia. In biblical times purple cloth was valuable, known to be worth its weight in silver. Purple was the color of nobility or royalty which indicates that Lydia was probably wealthy, otherwise she would not be able to afford her own inventory. It also meant she had a profitable business with a reputable customer base.

Lydia was a woman of prayer. So, although she operated a thriving business, she was also a planner who made sure there was time for things which she felt were important outside her business. It is unfortunate to see individuals get so wrapped up in their own productivity in business that they neglect to plan well for other areas which can enhance their emotional, relational, spiritual, or physical well-being. Lydia hadn't fallen into that trap.

According to Jewish law, a synagogue could not be formed unless there were ten male heads of households who could be in regular attendance. In the absence of this quota, a place of prayer under the open sky and near a river or sea could be established. There was no synagogue in Philippi at this time, so these folks were meeting by the river to pray. Here was a woman who was in the right place at the right time with a heart that was right before the Lord. Her heart was opened by the Lord to His truth. Once this happened, she had an immediate desire to use what she had for the furtherance of His kingdom. I believe this is evidence of a true relationship with Christ. Once our hearts are opened to the truth of the unearned grace and mercy offered to us through our Savior, the natural result is a desire to offer all we are and all we have back to Him.

Lydia's acceptance of Christ, her confession of Christ and baptism into the body of Christ played a significant part in the growth and development of the Philippian church. In Acts 16:40 we see that

Paul and Silas went to Lydia's house to meet with the believers and encourage them after they were miraculously released from prison in the middle of the night. Lydia's house became a home church: a nucleus of Christian ministry, fellowship, and worship.

Appropriate planning and prioritizing her time paved the way for Lydia's life to be transformed. As a result of that transformation, many other lives were influenced and subsequently radically changed for Christ.

A CHANGE OF PLANS

It is important to remember that the embracing of God's plan for us is not always easy, convenient, or even necessarily what we think makes sense. I'm sure that marching around the city walls seven times wasn't listed anywhere in Joshua's battle plans to infiltrate Jericho. My guess is that Jehoshaphat might have chosen a different strategy than sending the worshippers first into battle. Gideon probably would have felt more comfortable with more soldiers fighting against the Midianites, but God kept reducing the size of his army. In each of these cases, the plan of God was different from what made sense to the natural mind of man. But in each case, it was God's plan that led to victory.

Similarly the effects of failing to plan and the resulting consequences are well illustrated in God's Word. In the parable of the ten virgins (Matthew 25:1–13) only half the women showed up with full oil lamps and trimmed wicks. Before the bridegroom they were waiting for arrived, the five with near-empty lamps had to rush into town to try to buy more oil. They missed his arrival and could not go into the wedding because the doors were locked. How many times do we miss out on tremendous blessings due to lack of adequate preparation?

Even when we are required to wait on the fulfillment of a plan, having a plan can be a catalyst of hope. As the Lord spoke to Abram, He encouraged him with a visual reminder of His plan. In Genesis 15:5 (NKJV), we read:

> *Then He brought him outside and said, "Look now toward heaven, and count the stars if you are able to number them." And He said to him, "So shall your descendants be." The stars in the sky, the sand on the shore, constant and tangible reminders of God's plan for Abram even when in the natural what had been promised seemed impossible.*

When you remember that it was 25 years before Abram and Sarah had their son, Isaac, through whom the line of the Savior would come, any waiting we do seems minor by comparison.

FLIGHT PLANS

When we plan, we behave like our heavenly Father. A well-known verse that encourages many is Jeremiah 29:11:

> *"For I know the plans I have for you," declares the LORD, "plans to prosper you and not to harm you, plans to give you hope and a future."*

God has planned for us, so we must embrace the importance of planning. The amazing thing is that when we ask Him to reveal His plan to us, we can move into the Holy Spirit's jet stream based on His perfect flight plan.

Both of us have grown up in homes where our dads owned and operated private aircrafts. Planning is essential when you move from driving a car to flying a plane.

Not to negate good auto-care planning, but the reality is that when you have an engine failure or run out of fuel along a highway, there's a margin for error. The sky is not nearly as merciful and can become quite adversarial when proper planning is ignored.

As leaders in our homes, schools, and workplaces, we are called to a higher standard. We are called to pilot and ascend to a higher altitude in the hope of being the kind of leader that can give others the view from 30,000 feet. It's truly spectacular from that point of view. Things that seem so engrossing on the ground take on a whole new perspective from that height.

Wisdom tells us that we will never get off the ground without planning and, once we're in the air, we'd better know where we are going. Yes, there are times to relax and be without an agenda. Spontaneous trips can be fun and full of adventure, but unless you are going to "fly by the seat of your pants" — to sleep under the stars and rub sticks together in the hopes of igniting a campfire — even those trips need some planning.

It's wonderful when we can fly in a tailwind — it moves us to our destination quicker and with less effort. A headwind is just the opposite, but sometimes it cannot be avoided. However, when we plan ahead, study the forecast, and draw a flight plan that favors a less challenging route — it's a win/win.

THE IT FACTOR

■ PLANNING

> *The plans of the diligent lead to profit as surely as haste leads to poverty* (Proverbs 21:5).

"Good fortune is what happens when opportunity meets with planning."

—Thomas Alva Edison

- Planning is the process of prayerfully setting goals and then outlining the strategies, tasks, schedules, and resources necessary to accomplish goals. A plan has a big-picture vision as the aim with specific activities scheduled to achieve that vision. A plan is *not* a recap of what was accomplished in the past week.
- Planning never stops. If we want to achieve success, we must be in a continual state of preparation. Taking the time to plan gives us the opportunity to think with clarity about the vision, anticipate obstacles, and find the most efficient ways to use our time and resources.
- There is an old saying, "He who fails to plan, plans to fail." Without a plan, we are constantly reacting to situations rather than setting a course of action.
- Many people overlook or set aside planning and allow the demands of the day to guide them. They allow their focus to shift to the immediate needs, problems, or circumstances of their environment rather than focusing on the plan.
- Wise planning helps us to prioritize our commitments (keep first things first), eliminate time wasters and unnecessary tasks, and anticipate problems.

- While there are things that need to be attended to daily, the focus of activities should be connected *to* the plan rather than being a distraction *from* the plan.

■ QUESTION

Are your daily and weekly goals connected to your plan? Do you generally stay with your plan or do the activities and circumstances of the day dictate what gets accomplished?

■ BENEFITS OF PLANNING

You experience many benefits from prayerful and wise planning:

- You will experience achievement and God's blessing. You will be more productive and efficient, which will enable you to accomplish goals more quickly. You will not waste your time in areas where God did not intend for you to go.
- You will reduce the number of opportunities to be frustrated. Frustration is a symptom of blocked goals; it hinders progress.
- You will build momentum and morale. Great planning causes you to consider the situation from all angles so that you see the pitfalls or delays that could occur. By anticipating problems and having ready solutions or contingency plans, you can keep the plan in motion and continue to build on success.
- The important things will get done. By forming a plan and prioritizing needs, you ensure that your focus is on things that will bring desired results.
- You increase your value and open yourself up to new possibilities such as being promoted to higher levels or being given more important projects because you will have proven that you know how to accomplish both as an individual and as part of a team.

- You will build confidence in yourself because you will have a means to measure your success. You will also earn the confidence and trust of others.

Which benefit would you most desire to have? How do you see that benefit making a difference your life?

■ CHARACTERISTICS OF PLANNING

Here are some characteristics of people who are prayerful and wise planners:

- They have an aim in mind — a well-defined goal or vision they passionately desire to achieve.
- They set aside time for prayer and planning on a regular basis. They bring their ideas and opportunities before God before they act.
- They consult others on their plan. If they are married, they include their spouse in the discussion and respect their partner's thoughts and feelings on the matter.
- They have clearly defined short- and long-term goals with reasonable time frames in which to accomplish them.
- They make a list of resources needed to accomplish the vision including people, time, budgets, and materials.
- When the plan involves a team, they take the time to communicate the vision, update others on changes to the plan and ask people to contribute in their areas of strength. They encourage their team members and give credit and show appreciation for each person's contribution.
- They consistently take time to reflect and, when necessary, change the plan.

Do you know someone who demonstrates wise planning? What do you admire about that person? What must you do to be more like him or her?

■ PLANNING STEPS TO FOLLOW

Read the steps to follow below, and use them to develop a specific measurable action step to take this week.

1. **Plan to plan.** Carve out time for planning every week. Just because you aren't moving does not mean you aren't working. Taking the time to plan is work *and* it makes work time more productive.

2. **Determine and define the goal you want to reach.** Vision is the foundation of planning. If you plan without vision, you are merely creating a to-do list.

3. **Look at the situation from many angles.** Consider how the plan will affect you now and also in the future. Ask for input from your spouse, if you are married, and other people you trust. Proverbs 15:22 (*The Message*) reminds us, *Refuse good advice and watch your plans fail; take good counsel and watch them succeed.*

4. **Set your priorities.** Once you identify your specific goals, list them in order of importance rather than in the order of easiest things to do first. This will keep you focused and moving forward.

5. **Communicate the vision and plan thoroughly.** Many plans need to include other people. If this is the case, clarify the steps that need to be taken and, whenever possible, get their input. If you involve others in your plan, they will take ownership in it and more will be accomplished. Do not expect people to read your mind. Set them up for success by providing good guidelines and realistic time frames.

6. **Be aware of time wasters.** Either eliminate them or group them into blocks of time in your day to keep interruptions to a minimum.

This would include things like surfing the internet, running errands, watching television, email, filing, and unscheduled meetings.

7. **Evaluate your plan and make adjustments regularly.**
8. **Commit your plan to the Lord.** Pray before you plan, while you plan, and when you make adjustments. Ask God for His wisdom. Ask that He reveal your motives and His will to you.

> *Mortals make elaborate plans, but God has the last word. Humans are satisfied with whatever looks good; God probes for what is good. Put God in charge of your work, then what you've planned will take place* (Proverbs 16:1–3 *The Message*).

Share your specific action step. Remember to keep it specific by attaching a who, what, where or when to the statement.

_____

_____

_____

_____

_____

_____

_____

_____

_____

_____

_____

_____

CHAPTER 9

THE VALUE OF GENEROSITY

How does the Proverbs 31 woman fit in the category of generosity? Very simply. Although in some topics we might have to read into the text her characteristics, verse 20 states clearly, "She opens her arms to the poor and extends her hands to the needy." Obviously such generosity shown by the wife of one of the town's leaders also had contributed to her family's sterling reputation.

Are you a generous woman? When we follow the mandate of Matthew 10:8 (NLT), "Give as freely as you have received!", we practice the principle of generosity, which creates its own reward within our lives. Ultimately this reward is a satisfaction, which results from obedience as well as the knowledge that in some small way we have helped someone and given back to the Lord a portion of the good things He has given to us.

I think most of us tend to see ourselves as generous because it is human nature to view ourselves in a positive light. We know that to be generous is more socially acceptable than to be stingy, so we place ourselves in the most appealing category. Even when we are not generous with our monetary resources, we often consider the giving of our time, service, or expertise as something above and beyond what work, society, or even our family, requires. But what we sometimes fail to realize is that God sets the standard of generosity — not us — and certainly not the world in which we live. And the Lord always sets the bar higher than we do.

Our own nature tends to always want to operate within our comfort level. It's a self- preservation model. God, however, in the realm of generosity, pushes us to the very edge of our comfort level and urges us to take one more step. To give just a little more. A little more time than we think we have . . . a little more money than we think we can spare . . . a little more mercy than we feel inclined to offer. When we choose to do it God's way, we step out of the zone of *comfort* and into the zone of *faith*. We acknowledge that we just aren't sure how we are going to manage. We acknowledge that this may not seem like a very practical idea. We acknowledge that we are completely dependent on Him for things to work out well. And this is the very place where He desires for us to set up our tent and camp out.

OPEN-HOME GENEROSITY

Our friend, Tammy, like the Proverbs 31 woman, extended "her hands to the needy." She and her husband served as medical missionaries in Nepal, moving themselves and their children there for several years before returning to their medical practice stateside. There and in the United States, they have opened their hearts and home to minister to others in times of crisis. The physically challenged and infirm have found refuge and comfort in the Spirit-produced generosity they exhibit. We asked Tammy to share about one situation, and we believe it illustrates why she is a model for generosity for us. On a side note, this book would not have been written without Tammy's generosity in prayer support. However, prayer is just one of the many ways she has exhibited generosity in the real world.

Her philosophy of generosity is simple and biblically based. We are all called to be generous. She applies the truth of 1 Timothy 6:17–19 (*The Message*):

> *Tell those rich in this world's wealth to quit being so full of themselves and so obsessed with money, which is here today and gone tomorrow. Tell them to go after God, who piles on all the riches we could ever manage — to do good, to be rich in helping others, to be extravagantly generous. If they do that, they'll build a treasury that will last, gaining life that is truly life.*

Even more than knowing that God has promised good will come to those who are generous and lend freely (Psalm 112:5), Tammy knew that she had received the call of generosity. At one point that call involved opening up her home to a family of six in which the mother had just been given a terminal cancer diagnosis. She recalls that she and her husband, Rick, were at church for a special worship service. She was face down before the Lord, literally crying out for God to speak to her. She sensed that God was telling her to have that family move into their home during this time of illness and pending death. She felt called to provide emotional support and medical help to the ailing mother as well as practical help to other family members. Her husband readily agreed with what his wife was sensing from the Lord. Within the week, the family moved into their home. The ailing woman, Nancy, only had two months before she would go home to be with the Lord. Tammy recalls that those two months were filled with the peace of God and a calm confidence that affirmed the call to serve God by serving this family in need.

As we wonder under what circumstances we might be willing to add six people to our home, it seems clear that Tammy also exercised the gift of hospitality—a gift directly related to generosity. There is a Holy Spirit-inspired flow that comes with knowing that one is called to invite others in. Tammy says that it comes "without doubt or wringing the hands." It's not done under duress, and it's *not* considered an inconvenience.

Tammy also went above and beyond what many daughters-in-law in today's society do. Although she recognizes that her lifestyle affords it, she was thankful that she could assist in the care of her late father-in-law when he was given a diagnosis of terminal pancreatic cancer. She recalls having that same God-given assurance that she and Rick were called to be generous with their home, time, and compassion.

Of course, there are times when even the most generous become fatigued caring for someone in intense physical distress. However, knowing that God's heart is pleased with the sacrifice can strengthen our resolve to live with generosity.

OPEN-HAND GENEROSITY

In God's system, we all are equally commanded to give. This allows an entry-level teenager working at a fast-food restaurant and a chief executive officer (CEO) of a global corporation to be equally generous. They are both able to give their all, give nothing, or something in between. Yes, it looks a little different to the world; the CEO's gift to start a foundation will make the news while the fast-food worker's tithe placed in the offering plate won't.

If we were to place our measure of generosity next to Jesus, we would all fall short every time. Jesus modeled the ultimate act of generosity by giving His life on the Cross. And He did it for those who didn't even recognize His gift. Those who scoffed, beat, maligned, and eventually murdered Him were unknowing recipients of His limitless generosity — if they would receive it.

Of course, we are not capable of giving to the measure that Jesus gave. The life- giving resources that He possessed are beyond anything we possess. What we do have, however, is the ability to give to others much of what He has given to us. To take what He has offered us and offer it, with open hands, back to Him. When we give generously according to what we have been given, in obedience to the Lord and the leading of His Holy Spirit, we give in the same spirit as Jesus gave.

We often focus on the financial aspect when we speak of generosity, and the Bible does speak frequently about the subject. Jesus said that we cannot serve both God and money (Luke 16:13), so that's the bottom line. However, this Scripture has been misinterpreted to mean something it was never intended to. Throughout the Word, the Lord blessed many of His servants with wealth. In fact, without money, much good that could be done in the name of the Lord would fail to be accomplished. Churches planted, missionaries sent, the hungry fed . . . it all takes money. It's not money that is the root of all evil (as often misquoted), but "the love of money" that is the root of all kinds of evil (1 Timothy 6:10).

Those of us who have been blessed financially must be careful never to allow the money that we possess to possess us. This can display itself in different ways, as materialism, stinginess, or even in a workaholic attitude. When we allow our bank accounts to rule our lives and drive our actions rather than the Lord, we have created for ourselves an idol, fashioned not out of wood or stone, but out of the almighty dollar.

Keeping in mind that our ability to earn wealth (or even inherit it), lies in the hands of God will help us maintain perspective. James

1:17 reminds us, "Every good gift and every perfect gift is from above, and comes down from the Father of lights."

What are some of the good and perfect gifts He has given you? Have you taken an inventory of your resources lately? Every good thing you have within your life has Him as its source. Time, talent, treasure, mercy, grace, encouragement, and comfort — just to name a few. When we recognize that each thing we possess was given to us by God, we become more willing to allow Him to use these resources as He sees fit.

In a world so focused on materialism, it's easy to judge our own generosity, or that of others, by an earthly standard. God, however, has a different standard. True generosity is about holding every resource we possess with hands that are open to Him. It's about understanding that if He can trust us with what He has given us, then we can trust Him to provide everything we need. And it's about being aware that we have been offered the tremendous privilege of being a small part of accomplishing God's will on earth.

Generosity is not about what's in your wallet; it's about what's in your heart. It's about a lifestyle that says to the Lord, "Everything I have ultimately belongs to You to do with as You desire."

PASSING IT ON

If God has given us a great capacity for learning, do we generously and without pretense or pride, share the knowledge which we've been given? This doesn't only apply to book knowledge, but Word knowledge and life knowledge! Some knowledge cannot be embraced without great sacrifice of time, energy, and resources from the one who desires to receive. That being acknowledged, once we've gathered a harvest of knowledge, there are seeds that we need to set aside for replanting.

Being willing to invest our knowledge in others redeems the time we've invested, because then many can benefit from the toil of our brain and/or bank account. You may ask, "Why should others benefit from my hard work?" My answer would be, "Because you have benefitted from someone else's."

Both of us have been blessed in a practical sense as we have been given the opportunity to learn and grow from our parents' years of hard work in business. Our business sense is a legacy from our elders who allowed us to learn from their mistakes and saved both of us from unnecessary losses, financial and otherwise.

In a spiritual sense this applies as well. Those of us who have been blessed to have spiritual parents have been the beneficiaries of some of their knowledge of the Word. Because of the willingness of others to plant seeds in us, we now have the opportunity to plant seeds in others. In this way, the legacy of learning will continue. There are many examples of generosity demonstrated through *spiritual parenting* within the Bible.

Samuel spiritually parented David, Moses parented Joshua, and Elijah parented Elisha, to name a few. In each of these relationships a generous investment was made in both time and teaching. This investment resulted in a tremendous difference in the lives of those being parented. In 1 Timothy 1:2, the Apostle Paul made it clear that he considered himself a spiritual father to Timothy. Even though none of these men were related physically, there was a profound spiritual kinship.

If the Lord prompts you to invest in spiritually parenting anyone, do it in faith, trusting that He will help what you plant produce a good yield. Remember, He is the one who wastes nothing (John 6:12), so it is unlikely that He will direct you to plant in a field that has no ability to produce good fruit.

That being said, sometimes the Lord prompts us to invest in the lives of others, and we do not see the fruit produced that we desired right away — or sometimes ever. This can be discouraging. A lack of expected fruit does not necessarily mean we misinterpreted the Lord's leading regarding investing in that person. It could mean that we fulfilled our part but, for whatever reason, we may never see (on this earth) the results. Because the Lord never violates our will, there are those who will fail to take advantage of the generosity of time, wisdom, or resources given to them from the Lord through others. In these cases all we can do is to continue to pray for that person and trust God for the blessing of (eventual) obedience.

The ultimate example of spiritual parenting is Jesus who built into the lives of His disciples for three years. And those disciples "turned the world upside down" (Acts 17:6 NKJV) with the gospel message. Generosity is at its best when it can be multiplied. Jesus was a multiplier of epic proportions.

GIVING WOMEN

One of the greatest examples of generosity in the Bible was that of the widow who gave her two mites to the temple treasury. Even though it was very little in monetary value, it was *all* she possessed. We're told clearly that she was "poor." There was no credit card she could max out in an emergency. There was no pantry full of food she could live on, no savings account for a rainy day. Many people cling to a financial ledge of safety; she threw herself over in an act of total devotion. With a heart that was willing to give the Lord all that she had, this widow was said by Jesus to be far more generous than the rich who gave much more in monetary value. Her story is in Luke 21:1–4 (NKJV):

*And He looked up and saw the rich putting their gifts
into the treasury, and He saw also a certain poor widow
putting in two mites. So He said, "Truly I say to you that
this poor widow has put in more than all; for all these
out of their abundance have put in offerings for God,
but she out of her poverty put in all the livelihood that
she had.*

Although the widow was the epitome of giving, there are a number
of biblical accounts of generous women. It's likely that most of the
women cited in the Bible as positive examples were cited because
they were generous with their resources or their devotion or both. As
a traveling preacher, Jesus and His disciples lived partially through
the generosity of many women who contributed to their needs (Luke
8:2–3). Even the garment Jesus wore, that the soldiers at the Cross
gambled for, had been made seamlessly and beautifully by one of His
female followers.

Think of Mary of Bethany, the woman who anointed the feet of
Jesus with a very expensive perfume worth more than a year's wages.
The Scriptures (Mark 14:19) and our friend Elisha Morgan, who
teaches this passage so well, remind us that Mary "did what she could"
by lavishing this upon Jesus (v. 8). Although the stingy-hearted and
proud (especially Judas!) criticized her, Jesus honored her and said
that this gift was to be remembered forever, as it has been in the pages
of Matthew, Mark, and John.

All the money in the world could not compare with having the
privilege of anointing Jesus Christ. Mary knew the value of the gift she
gave but, through the eyes of love and faith, she saw the greater means
of blessing in her generosity. Christ was blessed and Mary was blessed
because *she did what she could.* Today I'm blessed to visualize in my

heart's eye the beautiful intimacy of that moment. As I write this, my heart swells with the desire to do what I can to honor Jesus with all that I have.

WHAT **WOULD** JESUS DO?

How does generosity of all types apply to our daily life? Take driving, for instance. How generous are you on the highway? Are you one that incites road rage in others because you drive selfishly? Do you wait until the last moment to get over simply because you are too impatient to wait in line like everyone else? Are you selfishly endangering others because you are not generous enough with your attention while behind the wheel? Texting while driving is fast becoming illegal in many areas. It's a tangible demonstration that our perceived need to share and receive personal information surpasses our concern for the safety of others. Let me just say this, if you choose to display a Jesus fish symbol on the back of your car, *please* make choices that demonstrate the love and generosity of Christ. Literally, *what would Jesus do*? If you are going to represent Him, represent Him well.

What if food manufacturers cut corners and lessened quality to increase profits, while knowing that their choice provided a less healthy and nutritious product? Would you consider that selfish or generous? Selfish, right? However, because we've been indoctrinated to look out for number one, self-centeredness is at an all-time high.

Much more seriously, the self-centered mentality of "me first, me only" has infiltrated society with horrendous consequences. Humans are being sex-trafficked because of this mind-set. That's a truth that cannot be denied. On the other hand, the kindness and generosity of others is swelling around the world to "put their money where their mouth is." Many are investing generously in efforts to rescue these precious ones (often children) from the torture of being used for the selfish and perverted desires of the debauched. May the generosity of those who have been made aware of this horrendous betrayal of humanity increase in strength, purpose, and resources.

BETTER TO GIVE

In the absence of the willingness of those in the body of Christ to receive the generosity of others, there is an inability of the system of God's economy to function properly. Would believers be encouraged to keep giving if every time they gave the potential recipient refused to receive what was offered? Although this rarely happens, there are cases. The unwillingness to receive what is freely given can be based on pride or fear. Pride says, "I don't want to give anyone else credit for what I have." Fear says, "I don't want to feel like I owe anyone anything." A clear understanding of how God works can help to defeat prideful or fearful thinking in this area.

The Lord often chooses to accomplish His will through His children. This takes many forms: Someone needs a word of encouragement? The Lord lays it on an individual's heart to call up that friend and encourage her.

Someone needs to be reminded of God's love for them? The Lord will lay it on someone's heart to unknowingly purchase just the right little gift that will directly communicate Christ's unique love to the recipient.

Someone prays that a financial need be met? The Lord will lay it on the heart of one of His children to meet that need.

For a child of God, little is more satisfying than knowing that you have heard from and been obedient to the Lord. There is confirmation for the giver when someone thankfully receives God-led generosity.

When we refuse to receive the generosity of others, we often deny them the opportunity to receive this satisfaction.

This can be illustrated in the simplicity of giving a compliment. Perhaps, in the midst of an ordinary day, you feel prompted to give a compliment to someone. They may have had a bad day or just need some encouragement. How this individual responds to your words can have varying impacts. Perhaps, they say something like, "Thank you so much! I was really having a bad day and that makes me feel a lot better." Then you might feel confirmation that you recognized correctly the inward prompting from the Lord, were obedient to it, and received pleasant feedback. Most likely, the result of this positive result will be that you will respond even more quickly to that inner prompting next time because you have experienced the rewards of obedience.

In turn, the individual who received the compliment will be blessed by your generosity and may have a desire to pass the favor on to someone else, after having experienced how something as simple as a compliment can make a positive difference.

> Mike, a friend of ours is a trainer for Global Priority, an organization that promotes taking values into the workplace by introducing a system where people meet one hour a week to discuss a value and determine a way to put it into practice. (It became the inspiration for our "IT Factor.") Mike was out of his homeland of Canada training a large organization in facilitating roundtable sessions on values. That particular day, they discussed with the group the idea of generously giving recognition. They asked each person to focus on sincerely giving recognition and compliments to others.

That evening, Mike and his fellow trainer, Nestor, went to dinner together. At the restaurant, they made it a point to treat the waitress with respect and to recognize how well she served them. At the end of the meal, she brought them their bill and they noticed it was not correct; she had only charged them for one meal. They kindly brought the error to her attention and she replied, "Oh, that was no mistake. I told my manager that you are the kindest customers I have ever had, and he told me to deduct one of your meals from the bill."

"Give and it shall be given unto you." Not only did Mike and Nestor receive a free meal, they had a great story to tell the people in the training session the next day about generosity in action.

Be forewarned that there are people with a works-based mentality who do not receive compliments well, especially if one seems (to them) undeserved. In these cases, the response to an unearned compliment is often argument or invalidation of the verbal generosity offered. When this happens, it can cause the one who gave the compliment to doubt if they were prompted by the Lord at all.

Of course, there are those who have the attitude, "I don't owe anyone anything—they're on their own. I have what I have because of *me*." After all, we live in a society that glorifies self-sufficiency and independence. One where the greatest value is found in being able to say, "I did it, all by myself!" Beginning when we are small children, we are praised as being *big girls* when we are able to accomplish something without help. Toddlers as young as age two proudly proclaim, "I do it *myself*."

I'm sure we've all met someone with an attitude which does not emote generosity. The grouchy person who wouldn't buy even one box of cookies from the cute little Girl Scout at the door? The Ebenezer Scrooge type. Often these are people who wish that things had been easier for them, that people had been kinder to them, that they had received generosity from someone along the way. For whatever reason, they did not receive much generosity and they resent it. They may have some achievements within their lives, but they feel that to get there was a tremendous struggle. They wear their independence as a badge pinned on by pride and bitterness. And they often adopt an "if I help you, I'm actually doing you more harm than good" mentality. Because they felt no one was generous to them, they withhold generosity from others. What individuals with this mind-set fail to remember is that we are not only called to act generously; we are blessed when we do. In Acts 20:35 (NKJV) Luke reminds us:

> *I have shown you in every way, by laboring like this, that you must support the weak. And remember the words of the Lord Jesus, that He said, "It is more blessed to give than to receive."*

When people think of you, what would you say is their first impression? Are you a giver? Or a taker? How do you see yourself? Why?

THE IT FACTOR

■ GENEROSITY

> *I tell you, love your enemies. Help and give without expecting a return. You'll never — I promise — regret it. Live out this God-created identity the way our Father*

lives toward us, generously and graciously, even when we're at our worst. Our Father is kind; you be kind.

> *Don't pick on people, jump on their failures, criticize their faults — unless, of course, you want the same treatment. Don't condemn those who are down; that hardness can boomerang. Be easy on people; you'll find life a lot easier. Give away your life; you'll find life given back, but not merely given back — given back with bonus and blessing. Giving, not getting, is the way. Generosity begets generosity* (Luke 6:35–38 The Message).

By feeding others, you will feed yourself.

- Generosity is giving without expecting anything in return. It is not based on our economic status, influence, or talent. It is giving from our hearts with the intent of benefiting another and is one of the best ways to show God's love to others.

> *This is how we've come to understand and experience love: Christ sacrificed His life for us. This is why we ought to live sacrificially for our fellow believers, and not just be out for ourselves. If you see some brother or sister in need and have the means to do something about it but turn a cold shoulder and do nothing, what happens to God's love? It disappears. And you made it disappear* (1 John 3:16–17 The Message).

- When we are generous, we are unselfish. We recognize we have the ability to have a profound effect on others. We give of our time, talent, and resources to serve others without thought as to what we will gain from giving or who will get the credit.

- As generous people, we have an abundance mind-set, not a scarcity mind-set. Proverbs 22:9 (AMP) says it like this: "He who has a bountiful eye shall be blessed, for he gives of his bread to the poor." We firmly believe there are more great ideas to be thought of and more fields into which we can sow. We are always looking for opportunities to add value to people or causes that will make a difference. We not only give when there is great need; we continually give because it is a fundamental part of our character.

- When we are generous, we value other people. We give but we also *forgive*. We consider others as we would like for them to consider us. We look for the potential in others, and then do all we can to help them develop it.

- We need to remember to be generous with those who are closest to us. Gifts can be special and meaningful, but small acts of kindness, our time, and attention can also go a long way to show appreciation and affection to those we care about.

- Generosity is helping people to believe in themselves and giving them the tools to overcome their circumstances and improve their quality of life. It gives people vision and hope. There is an old saying, "Give a man a fish and you feed him for a day. Teach him how to fish and you feed him for a lifetime." Generous people look for ways to help others gain the skills and resources they need for life.

- Generosity causes us to actively look for ways to invest in the development of a person or an idea. We recognize that there is more to life than acquiring money and that our wealth is only as valuable as what we do with it. We may be successful, but we become significant as we use what we have to positively impact others.

■ QUESTION

Which concept of generosity do you find most challenging? Do you struggle more with giving money, possessions, time, ideas, credit, or another aspect of this value?

■ BENEFITS OF GENEROSITY

If you practice generosity, you will experience these benefits:

- You will bring glory to God. Giving is an act of worship. Second Corinthians 9:12–14 (*The Message*) teaches:

> *Carrying out this social relief work involves far more than helping meet the bare needs of poor Christians. It also produces abundant and bountiful thanksgivings to God. This relief offering is a prod to live at your very best, showing your gratitude to God by being openly obedient to the plain meaning of the Message of Christ. You show your gratitude through your generous offerings to your needy brothers and sisters, and really toward everyone.*

- It simply feels good to be generous. You will boost your self-esteem and may experience an increase in your physical well-being. Medical studies have demonstrated that the positive feelings that come from generosity can strengthen your immune system and improve your emotional state. Knowing that you have, in some way, added value to another causes you to feel that you have been a part of something great.
- You will be better able to focus on the big picture in life and not be fixated on yourself. Putting the needs of others ahead of their own helps many people find a sense of direction. People healing from tragic or challenging events are often encouraged to invest in helping others because it helps them to maintain a positive focus and brings meaning to life.

- You will influence others to be generous. When someone is the recipient of another's generosity or is even just a bystander who witnesses it, he or she is effected in a positive way. This encourages him or her to also be generous.
- You will improve your relationships with those who are close to you. Being generous with your loved ones will create a happier and healthier environment where people feel appreciated and are more easily able to extend grace to one another.
- You will find the world opening up to you. Keeping a generous, global focus will give you a sense of a higher purpose and will bring experiences to you that you would never have had otherwise. You will open yourself to diverse experiences, cultures, and new people.
- You will reap what you sow. When you are generous with others, you will eventually receive generosity in return. While this should not be the motivation for giving, it is a nice benefit.

> *"The world of the generous gets larger and larger; the world of the stingy gets smaller and smaller. The one who blesses others is abundantly blessed; those who help others are helped"* (Proverbs 11:24–25 *The Message*).

Which benefit would you most desire to have? How do you see that benefit making a difference your life?

■ CHARACTERISTICS OF GENEROSITY

Generous people practice these traits:

- **They are unselfish**. Their thoughts are not consumed with how they can benefit but with how they can contribute to or add value to others.

- **They have a drive to make a difference.** Helping others is a high priority to them. They look for opportunities to assist others in developing skills that will enable them to support themselves and improve their lives.
- **They have an abundance mentality.** They believe that more can always be generated because **God** has provided the means for them to produce more with creativity and hard work. Deuteronomy 8:18 (*The Message*) gives a warning to those who think that abundance comes from within themselves:

> If you start thinking to yourselves, "I did all this. And all by myself. I'm rich. It's all mine!" — well, think again. Remember that God, your God, gave you the strength to produce all this wealth so as to confirm the covenant that he promised to your ancestors — as it is today.

- **They are compassionate.** They feel the needs of others and desire to help them find a solution.
- **They use what is in their hand.** They are willing to contribute whatever they have to benefit others. This may come in the form of advice, encouragement, time, sharing their talents, ideas, or knowledge or giving of their material possessions or finances.

■ QUESTION

Do you know someone you consider to be generous? What do you admire about that person? What can you do to be more like him or her?

■ GENEROSITY STEPS TO FOLLOW

Read the steps to follow below, and use them to develop a specific measurable action step to take this week.

1. **Look for the potential in others.** If you cannot see it, ask God to show it to you. Encourage them by believing in them. Commit to investing what you can to help them develop.

2. **Volunteer to help an organization in your community.** Find a cause you are passionate about, and look for things you could do to assist them. Make a decision to participate in solutions.

3. **Share your talent, knowledge, ideas, and experiences with others.** Make yourself available to your family, friends, and co-workers. This is a very practical way to be generous. If you are good at math, tutor a struggling student. If you sew, you could offer to fix a seam. Everyone is good at something. The options are endless.

4. **Be sensitive to the needs of others.** Put yourself in their places, and make an effort to understand them. Encourage them by suggesting possibilities and sharing hope.

5. **Be *quietly* generous whenever you can.** Do not call attention to yourself or make a public display with it. Let your generous acts speak for themselves and bring glory to God. Matthew 6:1 (*The Message*) warns us: "Be especially careful when you are trying to be good so that you don't make a performance out of it. It might be good theater, but the God who made you won't be applauding."

6. **Give financially to causes that you believe in.** Be willing to put your money where your heart is. And when you give, do it cheerfully as if you are giving it directly to God — because in a way, you are.

> *Remember: A stingy planter gets a stingy crop; a lavish planter gets a lavish crop. I want each of you to take plenty of time to think it over, and make up your own mind what you will give. That will protect you against*

sob stories and arm-twisting. God loves it when the giver delights in the giving. God can pour on the blessings in astonishing ways so that you're ready for anything and everything, more than just ready to do what needs to be done. As one psalmist puts it:

> *He throws caution to the winds,*
>> *giving to the needy in reckless abandon*
> *His right-living, right-giving ways*
>> *never run out, never wear out.*

This most generous God who gives seed to the farmer that becomes bread for your meals is more than extravagant with you. He gives you something you can then give away, which grows into full-formed lives, robust in God, wealthy in every way, so that you can be generous in every way, producing with us great praise to God (2 Corinthians 9:6–11 *The Message*).

Share your specific action step. Remember to keep it specific by attaching a who, what, where or when to the statement.

_____

_____

_____

_____

_____

_____

_____

_____

_____

_____

_____

CHAPTER 10

THE VALUE OF INFLUENCE

Think of a woman of influence in your city or community? How would you describe her? Would you say that she had a noble character worth more than royal jewels? Would you say that her husband and children took every opportunity to bless her name and praise her for her care of them and her home? Has she done such good works that she has even been praised at a city council meeting? The answer to those three questions concerning the Proverbs 31 woman was a resounding yes (described specifically in verses 10, 28, and 31). She was definitely an influential woman.

When I think about people who have influenced others in my lifetime, I think of the Cathy family that founded the Chick-fil-A franchise of restaurants. Their company, started about 1946, not only provides a very enjoyable product, but it has influenced the culture by remaining closed on Sunday while almost every other restaurant chain is open. They take the stand that the principle of Sabbath rest is biblical and, although they are open one day less than their competitors, they believe that those who value their stand will be even more apt to be a patron on the other six days each week.

We know this to be true. We live in what we call a "disadvantaged area" (note the tone of humor) in that we have to drive 30 miles to eat at a Chick-fil-A. And although we would love to be able to access their product in our local community, we don't take it for granted when we have the opportunity to pull into one of their drive-throughs Monday to Saturday. It's rather incredible how staying true to their mission not only has influenced generations but also affirmed that success is not always as culture would portray it. They give their workforce Sunday as a day of rest, and their employees return to work very customer service–minded when the doors are open.

Each week at our jobs, we take part in our respective company and/or community roundtables. The environment of mutual influence is one of the most appealing aspects of this positive habit. The hour a week that is invested by the persons involved is so often a *Sabbath* from the world's perspective on how to do life, faith, and business. We are all struggling in some area of life, but an hour of values-driven interaction can either directly address the big challenge or help to give perspective and positive solutions to the lesser challenges, thus affording time to focus and deal with the highest priority.

So often, without the influence of others, we are left to the inside-our-head emotions. There voices of doubt, condemnation, self-deception, and pride can abound. Communicating with others can help us understand that our best opportunity to influence a situation is when we can address the *need* first and not the *want*. Sometimes as employees we'd love to just fix the problem rather than discuss it, but then our influence as problem solvers wouldn't encourage a generational learning environment. We opt for influence because we know that even the least skilled or gifted individuals, if humble and teachable, can in turn influence thousands over the course of their lifetime and beyond.

MAKING THE CONNECTION

Have you ever walked through a grocery store and taken the time to smile at a stranger? Frequently, especially with elderly shoppers, the response I get is a smile with a surprised expression. Perhaps this is because in contemporary society we are so involved in our smartphones, iPods, and other electronic connection devices that we constantly miss opportunities to make a human connection.

I don't believe that we leave our homes planning to ignore everyone who crosses our paths. We have just become acclimated to a technology-driven disconnect that causes face-to-face communication to suffer miserably. In the checkout line where customers used to chat, both with the person standing behind them and with the cashier, they now have both their eyes and fingers busy texting someone far off. In the drive-through at the bank, tellers often have to wait for customers to pause their phone conversation long enough to accomplish their business, with no time for commonplace pleasantries. Airports and planes, identified as places where people hurry up and wait, once were hubs where strangers had the opportunity to become acquaintances and, sometimes, even friends. But today we can travel the width of the United States and be so consumed with our own toys and tools that we don't speak to anyone.

We have become so accustomed to communicating in an artificial manner that a handwritten card or letter seems a totally ineffectual use of time. Ironically, however, when we receive a personal letter, it's a pleasant surprise. Although we may be perplexed that someone, aside from our grandma, would communicate in such a provincial method.

I believe that people who really understand the value of influence know how to communicate in a way that moves the recipient to the next level of connecting, whether their message is sent by telephone call, handwritten note, or personal email.

BRANDED

Jesus had influence on others because He made the human connection. Being God, He understood exactly what was in the minds of people, and He knew how to connect in a relational way where positional power wasn't the focus. The high priest and his associates used their positions to try to influence the culture to reject Jesus because of His "radical" interactions with sinners. Many people, however, were influenced by the love, indisputable miracles, and life-changing truths that Jesus offered.

In today's marketplace, whether we are running a home business where we encourage others to purchase goods online or at home parties or we are engaging in corporate office environments, classrooms, or trade shows, there's a strong focus on *branding*. Products and programs come with a brand name. Companies that sell our educational system textbooks and achievement tests that are required in school districts all have a brand. It's this branding that sets apart the product, service, or person from the rest.

When you've had a positive connection to a brand, don't you become an advocate, either passively or assertively, for that brand? For instance, you may be using the same brand of detergent that your mother used because she swore that it was the best, you believed her and used it, and you may recommend it to others. Even within the church, we brand denominations, theological texts, styles of worship — you name it, we brand it.

In a more spiritual sense, brand equals reputation. A good reputation is often synonymous with influence. The Bible has much to say about the importance of an individual's reputation. Proverbs 22:1(NKJV) tells us, "A *good* name is to be chosen rather than great riches, loving favor rather than silver and gold." Our brand, our name, and our reputation all are important aspects of our ability to influence others. We must remember that the way we behave and the choices we make in both our words and actions can impact our ability to influence others. Are you known as someone who is reliable, trustworthy, kind? In the marketplace, is your *brand* of Jesus one that is preferable to the people He has called you to lead?

A WOMAN OF INFLUENCE

Talk about a biblical woman of influence and many thoughts go straight to the Book of Esther. Esther, a young Jewish woman, almost miraculously rose to the position of Queen of Persia.

When Queen Vashti refused an order from her husband, King Xerxes, to appear before a roomful of drunken men, the king didn't take kindly to the rebuff. Urged on by the men around him, who were afraid their wives might also decide not to obey them, the king deposed and divorced her. A countrywide search was made for the most beautiful young women so that the king could choose a new queen. Beautiful women were literally grabbed off the streets and taken to the palace. They could not refuse. When Esther was taken, it apparently wasn't known that she was a Jewess, part of a disliked immigrant population in Persia.

Through the workings of God behind the scenes, King Xerxes did choose Esther as his queen. She came into a position of wealth and comfort but not necessarily influence. Her job was to look pretty, make the king happy, and keep her mouth shut — unlike her predecessor. When her uncle informed her of a plot he overheard that, if carried out, would mean all the Jews would be killed, he begged her to intercede for them with the king. Esther was at first afraid but then decided to try to save her people, uttering one of the famous lines of the book: "if I perish, I perish" (4:16).

Through some clever moves (read the whole book to see her wisdom) Esther managed to show the king the true colors of Haman, who was plotting to kill the Jews, and to save her people from genocide. It's no wonder that every year Jews still celebrate the Feast of Purim, a memorial to the woman who saved them.

God put Esther in the right place at the right time to influence a king and spare thousands of lives. Our spheres of influence might not involve anything nearly as dramatic or dangerous. But we each have been put where we are to exercise God's will, to stand for what is right, to speak out against wrong. What Esther's uncle told her is true for us too: maybe you have been put where you are and given the position you have specifically "for such a time as this" (Esther 4:14).

POSITIVELY INFLUENTIAL

Leadership is based on our ability to influence. Mentorship is based on our ability to influence. Manipulation is based on our ability to influence. And yes, the third statement, although distasteful, is as true as the first two.

How are you using your influence? Are you using it to perpetuate positive change or emotional chaos? When someone hears your name, have you used your influence in such a manner that there's an instant positive response from those who have been around you? Or is there a cringe-effect, an awareness of how difficult you are to deal with?

There are many stories of positive influence in the Bible and thankfully none of them (except those about Jesus) involved perfect men and women. Even Saul, who had been such a negative influence in the earliest days of Christianity, was so influenced by Jesus Christ on the road to Damascus that he became the Apostle Paul, fully and contagiously converted to faith in Jesus. His life changed to such a degree that his Spirit-inspired words have influenced generations of Christ followers around the world.

How much influence could we have if we simply, like Jesus' apostles, allowed God to influence us to our depths? Are we using what God has given us through the death and resurrection of His Son to change the world? Are we actively being that salt and light that we are called to be? Are we asking God to use us to the depth of our personhood to influence and ignite transformation today in the lives of those around us? Do we even believe that He can . . . that He will?

Influencers demonstrate that "it can be done" and draw others to listen to their experiences. Influencers are willing to cheer others on with authenticity and transparency as they share areas where they once struggled but eventually were able to find success.

Thirsty people want a drink. Hungry people want to eat. That's human nature. If what we deliver into a situation is the message that Jesus is the Living Water, then we've set the table, pun intended, to invite the weary traveler looking to quench their thirst to come and drink. Same goes for the hungry. When you are really hungry and you smell something incredible, don't you want to eat? That is influence. We are to be that kind of influence in this world — the fragrance of Christ that causes others to desire to draw closer to Him. Second Corinthians 2:15–16 (NKJV) states:

> For we are to God the fragrance of Christ among those
> who are being saved and among those who are perishing.
> To the one we are the aroma of death leading to death,

and to the other the aroma of life leading to life. And
who is sufficient for these things?

When Jesus was speaking to the paralytic at the pool in John 5, He asked, "Do you want to get well?" At times we can influence someone with a simple question. Anyone who has been mentored, coached, or counseled knows this to be true. Those who know how to effectively influence others become skilled — not at telling others what they think or feel — but at asking the right questions. Drawing the truth out by questioning is more effective than simply telling someone the right answer.

Our level of achievement, either positive or negative, is predicated on whom we allow to influence us. The Word of God has much to say about this topic. First Corinthians 15:33 (NKJV) states that there are people whose influence we should avoid because "evil company corrupts good habits." Just as it is our responsibility to influence others with honor and integrity as the Lord leads us, we must be careful about those we allow to influence us. As Psalm 1:1–3 says:

> *Blessed is the one*
> > *who does not walk in step with the wicked*
> *or stand in the way that sinners take*
> > *or sit in the company of mockers,*
> *but whose delight is in the law of the Lord,*
> > *and who meditates on his law day and night.*
> *That person is like a tree planted by streams of water,*
> > *which yields its fruit in season*
> *and whose leaf does not wither —*
> > *whatever they do prospers.*

Traveling throughout central Europe, we see reminders of the influence of decades and even centuries. The acts of past generations influence the way individuals and countries view themselves. Horrendous acts that have become fibers in the fabric of a nation's history incite emotions, such as shame and regret, in its citizens. Likewise, acts of heroic rescue and justice increase the sense of patriotism, compassion, and activism in the hearts and minds of those who lay claim to that ancestral heritage.

> As a first-generation American, I have a deep sense of connection to the Swiss heritage of my dad. I find it compelling to hear the stories of how my dad would see refugees come into his country during World War II, seeking a safe place where they could escape the oppression and suffering of the Third Reich. These stories influenced me to embrace liberty and the freedom to worship as I choose. There's an incredible influence that the free have on the oppressed, and we should always preserve that privilege. Positive influence can be life-giving to the imprisoned.
>
> — *Lisa*

TO SEE A DIFFERENCE

Jesus, Caesar, Napoleon, Margaret Thatcher, Charlemagne, Hitler, Stalin, Gandhi, Muhammad, Solomon, Queen Victoria — each of them impacted the chronicles of history for good or bad. When, should the Lord tarry, people look back many years from now, how will you be remembered? Even if your name is not famous, will there be a chronicle of your involvement in the improvement of society? Will there be a little girl who goes to kid's church and finds she's a sinner in need of a Savior? Will the little girl have that opportunity because you invested in her ancestor at work who then became one of the leaders who planted a new church in her community?

Is it unrealistic to think that our presence on earth could impact someone we will never meet in this life — someone who has yet to be born? No. That's the miracle of influence. It's a precious gem to be treasured and worn with humility and wisdom.

Every time you turn on the evening news, you are witnessing how individuals choose to spend or invest their influence — from the retiree who volunteers to read to preschool students at the library, to those who donate blood at the Red Cross, to the police officer who guards against lawlessness, to the autoworker who signs off on the assembly line safety check. Each is an agent of influence in the area where he or she lives and works. Each is important and has the ability to be an integral part of God's plan.

Within the human heart there's a desire to make a difference. Depending upon how we leverage our influence in the marketplace, home, or educational arenas, we will see the effect of personal choices and how we embraced or rejected responsibility.

When I was a teenager, I dealt with a long season of sexual harassment (professionals termed it abuse) from one of my high school teachers. Due to the small community I was raised in, everyone knew everyone. Other students before me had encountered similar advances. Some received them, were discovered, and their reputation was marred. Some, I'm sure like me, rejected the advances and became an object to conquer as I was from my freshman year to graduation day. Those were years, and for many thereafter, of living in the shadows of those events.

Due to things that happen to us, we are often deceived into thinking that God cannot, or will not, use us. We become "angels with dirty faces." I'm living proof that even the most disturbing events can be part of our influence. I knew it to be true when

I sensed the call of God to women's ministry in 1998. Although at times it was deeply emotionally challenging to retell the story, I saw markers along the way that God was using my story. He allowed others to see that just because we've been victimized, we do not have to live as victims. Three decades beyond those events of high school, I see the truth in God using "all things" to bring good to us according to His purposes. It was never more clear to me than when I received notes from other women who had walked a similar path. I was given the opportunity to share my story and my influence on the national programs *FamilyLife Today* and *Chris Fabry Live!* and in television appearances with Babbie Mason and other media ministry leaders.

Our influence is so often shaped by our willingness to be honest with God, ourselves, and others. One of the most gratifying results of sharing my story is being able to share the influence that my friend Faith Jones had on my life. You'll remember in the chapter on the value of attitude (chap. 4) how Faith viewed and lived her earthly life. She had influence; she gave me the tools to heal my woundedness through the work of the Holy Spirit in her life. As a result, I have been able to share the influence of God on my life with women in several nations.

As much as the enemy of our soul wants to steal our influence, it is our choice as to whether or not we allow that to happen. If my influence and opportunity can be used to reveal truth to a friend, co-worker, or others I encounter, then suffering — whether deserved or underserved — is worth the pain of the journey. Jesus endured undeserved suffering to influence time and eternity. We should never doubt that a humble heart, submitted to God, can be used by Him to influence others in our world.

— Lisa

INFLUENTIAL LIVING

As songwriters, we know that the power of a melody and lyric to influence the thoughts, emotions, and motivations of others is huge! Sometimes hearing a song can change the course of someone's day. It's a privilege to be able to write songs that connect with people at the soul level and, if they are worship songs, in the depth of their spirit.

> One of the areas of influence that I am most thankful for and treasure is when I receive the privilege of leading others in worship. That is a time when God allows me to be a vessel to create an environment where others enter into the throne room and share intimacies with the Father. I consider it a tremendous blessing and a great responsibility. Each song is carefully chosen and practiced, I prepare the week before by delving into the Word, asking God to show me anything He wants me to share that might encourage others to worship Him and words that will help build their faith. I pray for my teammates and the people who will attend the service, and I also pray for myself that God would help me to empty my heart of me and to fill it with Him. To be honest, the best me anyone will ever see is during moments of worshipping God because that is when you will see the most of God in me. My aim in studying and applying God's values is that God will continue to transform me by the renewing of my mind so that the other areas I am given access to influence in will look the same as it does when I worship.
>
> — *Dawn*

An area of influence that is so often neglected is prayer. The influence we can have on generations to come is available as we "approach God's throne of grace with confidence" (Hebrews 4:16). Prayer is an incredible instrument in the hand, or should I say heart, of those willing to practice it. Our influence, skills, knowledge, and vision *are* important. However, we know through God's Word that we are limited. Thankfully, God is not. When we mix our influence with the prayer of faith on behalf of others, there's a supernatural door that opens for God's blessings to flow to both the one influenced and the influencer.

Our high school drama group recently performed *The Music Man*. In the play, the mayor who desires influence is constantly interrupted attempting to give an Independence Day speech. He repeatedly and pompously begins, "Four score and seven years ago — " while knowing that he doesn't have the level of influence that (the main character) con man Harold Hill has. But even the swaggering, self-promoting Hill eventually discovers that his influence is unsustainable because of his lack of character and integrity. That's when the scales fall from his eyes, and he embraces who he really is and whom he really loves. Meanwhile, the poor mayor has done nothing more than remind the audience of the incredibly enduring influence of Abraham Lincoln's Gettysburg Address!

The influence of Jesus is the yesterday, today, and forever type. What is so interesting about biblical characters, some of whom we've looked at in this book, is that society continues to reference the principle those characters teach us — whether their influence was good or bad. We must remember that God does not act like a dog trainer with His children. He doesn't always reward obedience immediately. But He will reward it ultimately. Truth and time do not always run hand in hand — some of the harvest of influence comes "in due season," as we're reminded in Galatians 6:7–10 (NKJV):

Do not be deceived, God is not mocked; for whatever
a man sows, that he will also reap. For he who sows to
his flesh will of the flesh reap corruption, but he who
sows to the Spirit will of the Spirit reap everlasting life.
And let us not grow weary while doing good, for in due
season we shall reap if we do not lose heart. Therefore,
as we have opportunity, let us do good to all, especially
to those who are of the household of faith.

The "household of faith" Paul talked about needs all the good influences it can get. With great sorrow, we recently heard the report of a couple in Christian leadership, known around the world, who lost their youngest child to suicide. This grief journey is one they had prayed they would never have to take. Not only did they have to deal with the pain of the loss, but they became the target of some ignorant and judgmental factions who seemed to rejoice in their sorrow. However, because of the influence they have, I firmly believe that God is using their influence in this dark and tragic season to glorify Himself. Seasons of grief remain, but their true influence will be felt as they have already begun to help and encourage others who travel this heartbreaking road.

THE IT FACTOR

■ INFLUENCE

Let me tell you why you are here. You're here to be
salt-seasoning that brings out the God-flavors of this
earth. If you lose your saltiness, how will people taste

godliness? You've lost your usefulness and will end up in the garbage.

Here's another way to put it: You're here to be light, bringing out the God-colors in the world. God is not a secret to be kept. We're going public with this, as public as a city on a hill. If I make you light-bearers, you don't think I'm going to hide you under a bucket, do you? I'm putting you on a light stand. Now that I've put you there on a hilltop, on a light stand — shine! Keep open house; be generous with your lives. By opening up to others, you'll prompt people to open up with God, this generous Father in heaven (Matthew 5:13–16 *The Message*).

The influence of good citizens makes society prosper.

- Through our natural interactions with others, we have the capacity to influence them daily. Influence is the power to affect the words, choices, behavior, development, or character of someone without the use of force or authority.
- As believers, our responsibility to influence is to be a testimony for Christ in all that we do, to develop godly character, and to draw the world to Him by demonstrating His love.
- Every one of us influences people every day. In John Maxwell's book, *The 360 Degree Leader*, he talks about leading from wherever you are in an organization — bottom, middle, or top. I think the same holds true with influence. You can influence positively from wherever you are if you are reflecting the behavior Jesus modeled and taught.
- Influence is leading people rather than driving them. Even if we find ourselves in a position of power and authority, we still need to lead people through influence as much as possible. Forcing an agenda,

by using our title or position, will breed rebellion and disrespect. Leading through influence requires patience and time but is the best way to create a long-term atmosphere of cooperation and productivity.

- Our sphere and degree of influence is primarily determined by our character, behavior, accomplishments, and how we relate to others — who we really are, not just who we say we are. People are more likely to listen to us and follow us when we show them respect and demonstrate authenticity, humility, and commitment.

- There is a powerful human desire for the chance to make a difference. Insecurity, self-doubt, anxiety, and timidity can prevent us from stepping out to make that difference. If we choose not to rise to the noble position of embracing our place of influence, we are walking away from God's calling and purpose on our lives. Paul talks of the importance of this calling in Ephesians 1:16–19 (*The Message*):

> *Every time I prayed, I'd think of you and give thanks. But I do more than thank. I ask — ask the God of our Master, Jesus Christ, the God of glory — to make you intelligent and discerning in knowing him personally, your eyes focused and clear, so that you can see exactly what it is he is calling you to do, grasp the immensity of this glorious way of life he has for his followers, oh, the utter extravagance of his work in us who trust him — endless energy, boundless strength!*

- Bottom line is everything we say, every attitude we employ, and everything we do has the potential to influence and affect those around us — even those we do not know well or at all.

■ QUESTION

Who are you influencing at this moment? Are you influencing them with the right attitudes and actions?

■ BENEFITS OF INFLUENCE

If you have influence with others, you will experience these benefits:

- You will have a chance to do something that makes a difference in the world.
- You will have the opportunity to share the vision God has given you and inspire others to pursue the calling God has on their lives.
- You will have strong, cooperative working relationships because people will respect you and want to succeed with you. Amos 3:3 (AMP) points out: "Do two walk together except they make an appointment *and* have agreed?" When you have strong relationships and influence with others, it will be easier to come to the place where you agree and can walk together.
- You will be able to accomplish more with others than you ever could have accomplished alone.
- You will naturally share what you are learning and feel the fulfillment of developing those around you.

Which benefit would you most desire to have? How do you see that benefit making a difference in your life?

■ CHARACTERISTICS OF AN INFLUENCER

People who influence others possess these traits:

- They are driven to do something that matters. They seek God for what His call is on their lives, and they are focused on being what He created them to be.

- They have a genuine concern for others. The success of those around them is just as important as personal success. Their relationships flourish as a result.
- They give others credit and show appreciation. They let people know what they value about them and encourage them in their gifts. This builds loyalty and favor. Proverbs 19:6 (ESV) tells us: "Many seek the favor of a generous man, and everyone is a friend to a man who gives gifts." Appreciation and recognition are valuable gifts and powerful influencers because they speak directly to hearts.
- They are accomplished in their field. Their level of development and achievement is attractive to the people that are around them. This allows them to develop a greater degree of influence.
- They look for opportunities to develop others. They want to share what they have learned so that they can empower and enrich the people around them. They embrace Proverbs 27:17 which states: "As iron sharpens iron, so one person sharpens another."

■ QUESTION

Do you know someone you consider to be an influencer of people? What do you admire about that person? What must you do to be more like him or her?

■ INFLUENCE STEPS TO FOLLOW

Read the steps to follow below, and use them to develop a specific measurable action step to take this week.

1. **Develop your character by basing your decisions and behavior on God's values.** Our ability to influence others is dependent on who we are and how we live. If our character is not attractive to others, our ability to influence them will be very limited.

2. **Seek the Lord.** Find out what God wants you to do and then start doing it. Stay focused and true to the call He has on your life. Have the courage to press on regardless of any setbacks or negativity you experience.

3. **Develop your knowledge and abilities.** Make the most of what you are good at. If you want to have influence on any team regardless of whether it is in a church, a business, or a civic organization, you must be knowledgeable and capable in order to establish your credibility with others.

4. **Be friendly and transparent.** Take time to let others know you care. If it does not come easy for you to genuinely smile and encourage others, make an intentional effort to do so. It may feel awkward at first but, over time, it will become as natural as breathing.

5. **Develop your relationships.** You must know the people around you well in order to affect them in a consistently positive way. Only by knowing them can you recognize and influence intangibles like energy, morale, timing, and momentum. If you spend time building relationships, you can develop a great degree of influence in any team or organization.

6. **Gain experience whenever you can.** Experience does not guarantee credibility, but it encourages people to give you a chance to prove that you are capable.

> *So let us seize and hold fast and retain without wavering the hope we cherish and confess and our acknowledgement of it, for He Who promised is reliable (sure) and faithful to His word.*
>
> *And let us consider and give attentive, continuous care to watching over one another, studying how we*

may stir up (stimulate and incite) to love and helpful deeds and noble activities (Hebrews 10:23–24 AMP).

Share your specific action step. Remember to keep it specific by attaching a who, what, where or when to the statement.

CONCLUSION

In each chapter of this book, we've talked a little about the Proverbs 31 woman who, with all her other attributes, was undeniably a worker. Like her, we all have *work* to do, whether that work takes place within the four walls of our home, a school, our church, or the marketplace. And in some of those places we may have roles of leadership. The values we discussed are all a part of leadership: understanding people, forgiveness, taking responsibility, having a good attitude, resolving conflict, showing restraint, being honest, planning well, being generous, and influencing others. You might even call them part of a godly work ethic.

Jesus is continually extending an invitation to walk with Him. But He also calls us to *work* with Him. He extends this offer to show us how He is able to accomplish His will through us. He doesn't want us to live a life filled with striving. He knows that striving only leads to exhaustion in all realms — spiritually, emotionally, and physically. In place of striving, He desires that we would do what He has called us to do, what can be done best when we rely upon Him for our strength and energy. He says to us today:

> *Are you tired? Worn out? Burned out on religion? Come to me. Get away with me and you'll recover your life.*

I'll show you how to take a real rest. Walk with me and work with me — watch how I do it. Learn the unforced rhythms of grace. I won't lay anything heavy or ill-fitting on you. Keep company with me and you'll learn to live freely and lightly (Matthew 11:28–30 *The Message*).

It's humbling, the realization that the Creator of the heavens and earth would allow us, mere humans, to colabor with Him in the process of seeing His will come to pass on earth. He could accomplish what He desires in any way He chooses and, yet, He has chosen me . . . He has chosen you. As Ephesians 2:10 (NLT) states, "For we are God's masterpiece. He has created us anew in Christ Jesus, so we can do the good things he planned for us long ago."

Remember in chapter 8 when we talked about planning? God is a planner and, when He was reviewing the plans He had for you, part of that plan was the good works He planned for you to walk in. To be that bright light that shines in the darkness of this world. To be the salt of encouragement and truth that has the potential to influence and impact others. What is your calling? To be salt and light — plain and simple.

Perhaps you're thinking: *Me? God would really never want to use me for something as important as that.* If so, somewhere along the way you began to believe the whispers of the enemy. The one who in Genesis asked Eve, "Has God really said . . .?" The enemy would like nothing more than to convince each of us through accusations, condemnation, and deception, that somehow we have disqualified ourselves from being salt and light on the earth. When those thoughts come we must be diligent to remember, as 2 Corinthians 10:4 (NKJV) says, that "the weapons of our warfare are not carnal but mighty in God for pulling down strongholds." And in verse 5 we are told exactly how to battle such thoughts: by "casting down arguments and every high thing that exalts itself against the knowledge of God, bringing every thought into captivity to the obedience of Christ."

How do we bring every thought captive to the obedience of Christ? By making sure that what we are thinking aligns with the truth of God's Word. The only way to do this is to fill ourselves with His Word so that we will be able to immediately either recognize thoughts as part of the truth that we know or cast them away because they cannot be reconciled with what we know about Christ. Do not allow yourself to be deceived.

> *You have been called.*
> *You have been chosen.*
> *You have been set apart for such a time as this.*

LIVING OUR VALUES

Increased political correctness unfortunately neutralizes the words we are allowed, by law, to share in many marketplace or educational environments. Most of us turn on the news and are disillusioned by the direction our society is going. The freedoms we now possess are slowly but surely slipping away like sand in an hourglass.

For decades, Christ followers have depended so heavily on words, that actions and character have sometimes suffered in places where freedom of speech has been the pinnacle of society. Although many would like to believe that some of our freedom remains, we are becoming more and more aware of its absence. The good news is that this has come as no surprise to our God, and Jesus has not fallen off the throne. In fact, it was Jesus who said, "In this world you will have trouble but take heart! I have overcome the world" (John 16:33).

Most of the world knows what Christians stand for and many of the things that we say we believe. They know what we think is wrong or right. They know how we think they should live and what we think they should or shouldn't do. The problem is that our lives may look no different from theirs in many ways, except served with a side of judgment. A lack of grace, coupled with a harsh opinion about the sins of society, and a failure to show love doesn't showcase the qualities of either salt or light.

As believers, we cannot live like those we are condemning in the world, carry as much emotional baggage as they do, and expect the world to want to embrace the God we claim to serve. Until we are willing to live by the truths that we say we believe — until we are ready to be "Jesus with skin on" to both our friends and our enemies — we can expect the negative reactions we will sometimes get.

This is the reason we believe so strongly in the values we've written about in this book. We believe that *igniting transformation* is something that is beyond words. It comes through the choice to live a life of principle, to be, as Jesus said we should be, *in the world* but not *of it*. When people see that we display biblical values within our lives on a daily basis, they will take notice. Without even saying a word, the difference will speak volumes of a love and peace that the world does not know.

Remember: Thoughts become actions. Actions become habits. Habits become our destiny.

So then, how should we live? The Apostle Paul cites the character development of the Christ follower in Romans 5:3–5. *The Message* translation helps us process this truth in a contemporary, conversational manner:

> *There's more to come: We continue to shout our praise*
> *even when we're hemmed in with troubles, because we*

know how troubles can develop passionate patience in us, and how that patience in turn forges the tempered steel of virtue, keeping us alert for whatever God will do next. In alert expectancy such as this, we're never left feeling shortchanged. Quite the contrary — we can't round up enough containers to hold everything God generously pours into our lives through the Holy Spirit!

The generations before us acted in ungodly ways. Our generation acts in ungodly ways, and the generation that is coming behind us acts in ungodly ways. So some would say, "Why bother?"

Quite simply, because until Jesus Christ returns there will always be a remnant of people appointed to be salt and light in their generation. The environments may change, but the message remains the same.

The amazing thing about living a principled life is that it translates into any environment. Truth is truth. Truth does not change because the societal moral standard is legislated to accommodate the whims of the public. And, as hard as humanity tries to negate the reality of truth, there's always someone, somewhere who can *see* that the world system is broken. For as long as this world exists in its present state, sin will damage the hopes, health, and welfare of the human race. If this were not so, then Jesus Christ would not have suffered and died. It's just that simple.

That's why the message of grace through faith is so precious to those who have embraced His amazing grace. Its sound is sweet to the wretch that has been rescued from the penalty of eternal separation from a Holy God. And those of us who know that sweetness — who have tasted and seen — have the tremendous privilege to now share that sweetness with others.

The values that make Jesus Christ the unique Savior have been birthed in us because we've become members of His family through adoption. Because He lives, we can live in a way that not only pleases God, but influences others to want what we have been given through our love relationship with Jesus. Romans 12:2 (NLT) states:

> *Don't copy the behavior and customs of this world, but let God transform you into a new person by changing the way you think. Then you will learn to know God's will for you, which is good and pleasing and perfect.*

We wrote a song together a few years ago that reflects a life transformed by a relationship with Jesus Christ. This lyric tells the story of a woman who, until she met Jesus, had lived an unprincipled life. Poor choices had left the woman at the well (who we talked about in chap. 1) vulnerable to societal shame and isolation. How many contemporary conversations might have some similar themes running through them — spoken and unspoken words and emotions of those whom we see all week? Can you see the faces of the women in your sales department? Teacher's meeting? Courtroom? Neighborhood grocery store? Sporting event at school? What are they telling you? Based on John 4:

> *Walking in a shadow land*
> *Of broken dreams and shifting sand*
> *'Cause I gave my heart away too many times*
> *I didn't plan to meet You there*
> *Your kindness took me by surprise*
> *When grace and mercy showered over me*
> *Now I live to praise*

I live to praise you
The Father's heart is full of love for me
I live to praise, I live to praise You
The Lover of my soul has set me free

Is this the message that women in your workplace are dying to hear? Do you encounter hurting, broken, confused, and wounded women daily or weekly? Igniting transformation is a solid, truth-based launch pad for an incredible journey into the heavenly places where God calls us to fellowship with Him. Values and principles give us a language to speak to every person regardless of economic circumstance or belief system. Truth transforms — there's no way around it.

Join us as we take this faith journey. The road stretches out before us, and Jesus is ready to walk it with us.

What a God! His road stretches straight and smooth. Every God-direction is road-tested. Everyone who runs toward him makes it (Psalm 18:30 *The Message*).

Resources to strengthen the leader in you!

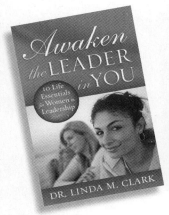

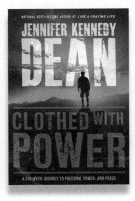

Awaken the Leader in You
10 Essentials for Women in Leadership
DR. LINDA M. CLARK
ISBN-13: 978-1-59669-221-3
N084144 • $12.99

Clothed with Power
A Six-Week Journey to Freedom, Power, and Peace
JENNIFER KENNEDY DEAN
ISBN-13: 9 978-1-59669-373-9
N134114 • $14.99
*DVD study also available

Journey to Confidence
Becoming Women of Influential Faith
KIMBERLY SOWELL
ISBN-13: 978-1-59669-389-0
N134130 • $14.99

Unlocked
5 Myths Holding Your Influence Captive
CYNTHIA CAVANAUGH
ISBN-13: 978-1-59669-385-2 • N134126 • $14.99

Available in bookstores everywhere. For information about these books or our authors, visit NewHopeDigital.com. Experience sample chapters, podcasts, author interviews and more! Download the New Hope app for your iPad, iPhone, or Android!

Visit our new online women's Bible study community at NewHopeDigital.com/women. Engage with our world-renowned Bible study authors, read relevant articles, blogs, and content for women of all ages, and deepen your walk with Christ through our new digital interactive Bible study workbooks.